love your library

Buckinghamshire Libraries

0845 230 3232

www.buckscc.gov.uk/libraries

24 hour renewal line

0303 123 003

easy COOK
express

OVER 100 QUICK RECIPES FOR BUSY PEOPLE

Edited by Sarah Giles

BOOKS

Contents

Introduction

Easy Cook magazine does exactly what its title suggests – it makes cooking easy! And this cookbook is designed to show you just how straightforward making home-cooked meals can be.

From beginner cooks who want to build up a repertoire of failsafe recipes, through to those who are much more experienced in the kitchen but need some new inspiration, the *Easy Cook* magazine team always aims to make sure that our mix of recipes appeals to as many people as possible. In this new book we've brought together some of our very best ideas – it's a bit of cliché, but you'll find something for everyone here. Most importantly, all the recipes we've chosen have got one thing in common: they're really quick to make. 'Express' cooking is the name of the game here!

If you want to get healthy, tasty food on the table every night without any fuss, this is the book for you. We want to show you that it's perfectly possible to cook from scratch using fresh ingredients, without spending hours in the kitchen. Someone once said to me that having a copy of *Easy Cook* to hand when you're cooking feels as though you've got a fun and knowledgeable friend with you in the kitchen, and that's exactly how we hope you'll feel about your copy of *Easy Cook Express* too.

We start off with Easy Everyday Food, inspired by the section of the same name in the magazine. It centres on our flagship 'Fast Meals for Weeknights' feature, and all the recipes you'll find here can be on the table in 20 minutes or less. Most of them can easily be scaled up or down, depending on how many people you're cooking for, and they include plenty of ideas for the ingredients you probably buy week in, week out. If you find you always tend to make the same old dishes, you're sure to find something new to try here.

Easy Family Favourites is designed to help get the whole family back round the table for a meal, even if other commitments mean that's only possible a couple of times a week, while our Easy After-School Suppers are perfect for when it's just the kids and their friends you're cooking for, and even fussy eaters will be happy!

There are ideas for packed lunches too, because we know how hard it can be to think of new things to put in lunchboxes every day whether they're for you to take to work or for the children to take to school. Got ingredients left over in the fridge? Try the ideas for using up anything from the last few spoonfuls in a jar of pesto, to a mound of mashed potato or leftover green veg. And as the week draws to a close, turn to Easy Friday Night Takeaways and try a delicious homemade alternative to your usual take-out meal.

Easy Weekend Food is the section to turn to when you've got a little more time. Preparation of the recipes won't take much more time, but recipes may need a little longer in the oven here. There are some fabulous roasts (with all the trimmings, of course) in Easy Sunday Lunches, with delicious puds to serve afterwards. You'll find ideas for eating out of doors on lazy summer days too – choose from our barbecue ideas or head off for a picnic in the sun.

Start your weekend in decadent style with one of our lovely brunch ideas. What could be nicer than whiling away a morning with the weekend papers and a pile of ricotta pancakes dripping with honey, or some eggy bread dipped in a tangy salsa?

Are you cooking for a celebration or special occasion? We've got a fantastic chocolate birthday cake for you, not to mention some

fab canapé ideas to serve with drinks, and two super-delicious puddings that work beautifully on a party buffet table. At Christmas, our turkey recipe is one that everyone should have in their repertoire, and there's a clever twist on traditional mince pies and some cute *Christmas pud cupcakes* as well.

For those who love to bake, our *Marbled chocolate brownies* will quickly become firm favourites, and the *Mango and passion fruit roulade* looks really impressive (but we won't tell anyone how easy it is to make, if you don't).

If you're planning to invite friends over for a meal, our ideas for starters, main courses and desserts won't let you down. How does *Scallops with fresh tomato sauce*, followed by *Pan-fried pork with crème fraiche*, then *Strawberry vanilla tart* sound? And if you're after something a bit more casual, cook *Prawn and tomato spaghetti* and everyone will be asking you for the recipe!

Happy Cooking!

Sarah Giles
Editor
Easy Cook

PART ONE

easy everyday food

Great recipes for midweek meals, to take you through from Monday to Friday

Our mission is to prove that it's possible to rustle up a great-tasting homemade meal in not much more time than it takes to zap a ready meal in the microwave or call for a takeaway.

The recipes in this section all take little time to make, and they use common ingredients that you'll find in any supermarket, along with storecupboard items that you're likely to have in the house already. There are no fancy cooking techniques involved and our clear, step-by-step instructions make the recipes straightforward to follow.

Whether you want to cook with meat or fish, or you're looking for vegetarian ideas, we hope you'll find something to tempt you here. We've got lots of easy weeknight suppers, as well as meals you can pack up to take to work for lunch (or that the children can take to school). There are recipes that are perfect for when the kids bring friends home for tea, and meals to encourage the whole family to sit down to eat together as well as plenty of ideas for using leftovers up too. Enjoy!

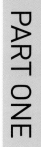

Pork with five-spice and cashews, page 22

easy
SUPPERS
ready in 20 minutes or less

All the inspiration you need for tasty weeknight meals that can be on the table in no time at all.

You've come home from work late, and you're tired and hungry. You know you should eat a healthy meal, but you open the fridge, can't think what to do with any of the ingredients in it and decide it's easier to just pop a ready meal in the microwave. We know the feeling, we've all done it and it's fine every now and again, but it's all too easy to slip into the habit of relying on ready meals when you're busy.

Or maybe you've just got back from ferrying the children around to their various after-school activities and everyone's fractious because they're hungry. What do you do? In the time it takes for that takeaway to arrive or to wait for the microwave to ping, you could rustle up something healthy, tasty and nutritious that everyone will love.

To help you, we've taken shortcuts where possible; there's nothing wrong with using a sachet of stir-fry sauce, for example, if it's going to encourage the family to wolf down the veg that's in the recipe too!

Tomato and thyme cod, page 19

Sticky cashew chicken with beansprout salad

Chilli oil gives this a real kick but you can use olive oil if you prefer a milder flavour. Squeezing lime juice over at the end gives a delicious sweet-sour taste to the finished dish.

- Serves 4
- Ready in 15 minutes
- Not suitable for freezing

2 tbsp soy sauce
3 tbsp clear honey
4 skinless chicken breasts, cut into strips
1 tsp olive or chilli oil
100g cashew nuts
100g baby leaf spinach
1 bunch spring onions, sliced
150g beansprouts
juice of 1 lime
a little olive oil, for drizzling

1 Mix the soy, honey and chicken, and leave for 5 minutes. Heat the oil in a wok or frying pan. Stir-fry the chicken and nuts for 3–4 minutes. Turn up the heat and cook for 3 minutes more, until the honey turns sticky and coats the chicken.

2 Mix the spinach, spring onions and beansprouts in a bowl. Drizzle with the lime juice and olive oil, then season.

Serve with lime wedges.

Oriental beef skewers

You can vary the flavour of this by using different stir-fry sauces, but oyster and spring onion works particularly well. If you're using wooden skewers rather than metal ones, soak them for as long as you can before cooking to prevent them from burning.

- Serves 4
- Ready in 15 minutes
- Not suitable for freezing

4 thin-cut sirloin steaks or minute steaks, trimmed of any fat and each cut into 3 long strips
120ml sachet stir-fry sauce (we used oyster and spring onion)
1 tbsp sesame seeds
1 tsp white wine vinegar
1 tsp light soy sauce
1 cucumber, cut into small chunks
3 spring onions, sliced
½ red chilli, deseeded and finely chopped
handful of coriander leaves, chopped

1 Heat the grill to high. In a bowl, mix the steak strips with the stir-fry sauce and sesame seeds. Thread onto 12 skewers, then grill for 6 minutes, turning halfway through, until golden and sticky.

2 For the salad, mix the vinegar and soy sauce together, then toss with the cucumber, spring onions, chilli and coriander.

Serve with steamed rice.

Salmon with warm chickpea salad

Covering the grilled peppers with cling film makes it really easy to peel off the bitter skins. This salad works well with lentils or beans, instead of chickpeas.

- Serves 2 (easily multiplied)
- Ready in 20 minutes
- Not suitable for freezing

1 large red pepper, deseeded and quartered
grated rind and juice of ½ lemon
pinch ground smoked paprika
1 tbsp olive oil
100g pack baby spinach leaves
two 140g skinless salmon fillets
400g can chickpeas

1 Heat the grill. Squash the pepper quarters flat and grill for 5 minutes, or until blackened. Leave the grill on, then transfer the peppers to a bowl, cover with cling film and leave to cool slightly before peeling off the skins and cutting the flesh into strips.

2 Make the dressing by whisking together the lemon rind, juice, smoked paprika, olive oil and seasoning. Toss half the dressing with the spinach leaves and divide between 2 bowls.

3 Season the salmon and grill for 5 minutes, or until just cooked through. Meanwhile, heat the chickpeas and their liquid in a pan for 3–4 minutes. Drain well, then mix with the remaining dressing and strips of pepper. Spoon over the spinach and top with the salmon fillets to serve.

Gnocchi with creamy tomatoes

This is lovely just as it is, but you can spice it up by adding a pinch of dried chilli flakes to the chicken before cooking, if you like.

- Serves 4
- Ready in 15 minutes
- Not suitable for freezing

2 cloves of garlic, crushed
1 tbsp olive oil
400g can chopped tomatoes
140g mascarpone
500g pack gnocchi
200g bag of baby spinach leaves
handful of basil leaves
parmesan shavings, to serve (optional)

1 Fry the garlic in the oil until golden, add the tomatoes, season, then simmer for 10 minutes. Stir in the mascarpone and cook for 2 minutes more.

2 Meanwhile, cook the gnocchi according to pack instructions. Add the spinach for the final minute of cooking. Drain, return to the pan, and stir in the sauce.

Serve with basil leaves and parmesan shavings scattered over, if you like.

10-minute pad Thai

For a vegetarian version, try fried tofu and thinly sliced pepper in place of the prawns. This is a super-speedy supper – and, best of all, it's all cooked in one pan.

■ Serves 2 (easily multiplied)
■ Ready in 10 minutes
■ Not suitable for freezing

200g raw peeled prawns
small pack coriander, stalks finely chopped, leaves roughly chopped
two 200g packs straight-to-wok pad Thai noodles (or dried noodles cooked according to pack instructions)
85g beansprouts
1 egg, beaten
juice of 1 lime, plus wedges to serve
1 tbsp fish sauce
2 tsp sugar
1 tbsp roasted peanuts, roughly chopped

1 Dry-fry the prawns and coriander stalks in a non-stick frying pan for 1–2 minutes, until the prawns are just pink. Add the noodles, beansprouts, egg, lime juice, fish sauce and sugar. Quickly toss together for 1 minute more, until the egg is just cooked and everything is well mixed – using a pair of tongs makes this easier.

2 Remove from the heat, mix in most of the coriander leaves, then divide between 2 bowls. Scatter with the remaining coriander and the peanuts.

Serve with lime wedges for squeezing over.

Creamy sausage and rocket linguine

A great way to ring the changes with sausages for a midweek meal. Deseed the chillies for a milder flavour, if you like.

■ Serves 4
■ Ready in 15 minutes
■ Not suitable for freezing

8 pork sausages
2 tsp olive oil
400g linguine
100g rocket
1–2 red chillies, finely chopped
150ml single cream

1 Squeeze the sausage meat out of the skins and break into small chunks. Heat the oil in a frying pan. Fry the sausage for 8 minutes, or until crisp and golden.

2 Meanwhile, cook the pasta according to pack instructions and chop most of the rocket. Add the chilli to the sausages, fry for 30 seconds, then tip in the cream and chopped rocket. Season and heat until the rocket just wilts.

3 Drain the pasta, reserving some of the cooking liquid, then mix the sauce through the pasta with a splash of the reserved cooking water. Top with the remaining rocket.

Lamb steaks with tomato and courgette crush

Don't be tempted to miss out the stage of squeezing excess water from the courgettes – it only takes a minute, and will make a big difference to the flavour and texture.

- Serves 2 (easily multiplied)
- Ready in 20 minutes
- Not suitable for freezing

2 courgettes
2 tbsp olive oil
2 cloves of garlic, chopped
10 cherry tomatoes, halved
handful of chopped parsley or coriander
2 lamb leg steaks

1 Chop the courgettes into large chunks, then boil or steam until tender (about 5 minutes). Tip into a colander and lightly press out as much liquid as possible using a potato masher or fork, then chop the courgettes into smaller pieces.

2 Heat the oil in a pan, add the garlic and tomatoes, then fry briefly until the tomatoes are just softening. Stir in the courgettes and heat through, then add the chopped parsley or coriander and stir through. Keep warm.

3 Season the lamb steaks and grill for 3–4 minutes on each side.

Serve with the tomato and courgette crush on the side.

Tomato and thyme cod

This is one of those great dishes where it tastes as though a lot more effort has gone into making it than actually has! The rich, tasty sauce thickens up beautifully and the fish takes up extra flavour from it while it's cooking.

- Serves 4
- Ready in 20 minutes
- Suitable for freezing (if fish is previously unfrozen)

1 tbsp olive oil
1 onion, chopped
400g can chopped tomatoes
1 tsp soft light brown sugar
a few thyme sprigs, leaves stripped
1 tbsp soy sauce
4 cod fillets (or another white flaky fish, such as pollack)

1 Heat the oil in a frying pan, add the onion, then fry for 5 minutes until lightly browned. Stir in the tomatoes, sugar, thyme and soy, then bring to the boil. Simmer for 5 minutes, then add the cod. Cover and simmer for 8–10 minutes, until the cod flakes easily.

Serve with baked or steamed potatoes.

See photo on page 10

Feta tabbouleh with aubergines

If you take your lunch to work every day, it's worth making double the quantity so you've got enough for your lunchbox too. Any leftovers make a great side salad too.

- Serves 4
- Ready in 20 minutes
- Not suitable for freezing

140g bulghar wheat
2 cloves of garlic, crushed
4 tbsp olive oil
2 aubergines, thinly sliced
    lengthways into strips
400g can chickpeas, rinsed and drained
140g cherry tomatoes, halved
1 red onion, chopped
100g feta, crumbled
1 large bunch mint, leaves chopped
juice of 1½ lemons

1 Cook the bulghar wheat according to pack instructions, then drain well. Mix together the garlic and olive oil, then use half to brush over both sides of the aubergine strips. Season. Sear the strips on a hot griddle or in a frying pan for 3 minutes on each side, until charred and softened.

2 Tip the bulghar wheat into a large bowl with the chickpeas, tomatoes, onion, feta and mint, then pour over the remaining garlicky oil and the lemon juice. Mix and season well, then pile onto plates with the charred aubergines.

Summer eggs

If you don't have any fresh basil to hand, stir a couple of teaspoons of pesto into the pan before adding the eggs.

- Serves 2 (easily multiplied)
- Ready in 15 minutes
- Not suitable for freezing

1 tbsp olive oil
400g courgettes (about 2 large ones),
    chopped into small chunks
200g pack cherry tomatoes, halved
1 clove of garlic, crushed
2 eggs
few basil leaves, to garnish

1 Heat the oil in a non-stick frying pan, then add the courgettes. Fry for 5 minutes, stirring every so often until they start to soften, add the tomatoes and garlic, then cook for a few minutes more. Stir in a little seasoning, then make two gaps in the mix and crack in the eggs.

2 Cover the pan with a lid or a sheet of foil, then cook for 2–3 minutes until the eggs are done to your liking. Scatter over a few basil leaves and serve with crusty bread.

Prawn and coconut laksa

Coconut milk is one of our favourite 'magic ingredients' – it immediately adds an exotic flavour to a recipe. This is a lovely, quick meal to eat on a cold day.

- Serves 2 (easily doubled)
- Ready in 15 minutes
- Not suitable for freezing

2 tsp oil
2 cloves of garlic, crushed
2 spring onions, finely chopped
2 tsp finely chopped fresh
**   root ginger**
1 large green chilli, deseeded
**   and finely chopped**
juice of 1 lime
200g raw peeled prawns
400ml can coconut milk
200ml chicken or vegetable stock
200g dried egg noodles

1 Heat the oil in a large pan or wok. When hot, add the garlic, spring onions, ginger and green chilli. Cook on a medium heat for 3–4 minutes, and then add the lime juice.

2 Stir in the prawns, then add the coconut milk and stock. Simmer gently for 5 minutes, until the prawns are pink.

3 Meanwhile, cook the egg noodles according to pack instructions. Drain, then add to the prawn and coconut mixture. Season to taste.

Serve with chopped coriander, if you like.

Pork with five-spice and cashews

This works really well with tofu in place of the pork, if you're cooking for a vegetarian. The drizzle of sesame oil at the end isn't essential, but if you have some in the cupboard already it does add an extra layer of flavour.

- Serves 2 (easily multiplied)
- Ready in 20 minutes
- Not suitable for freezing

2 lean pork steaks, cut into strips
2 tsp Chinese five-spice powder
2 tbsp vegetable oil
1 red chilli, sliced
½ bunch spring onions, chopped
1 yellow pepper, deseeded and cut into large
**   chunks**
150g crunchy veg, such as baby corn,
**   mangetout or sugarsnaps**
50g cashew nuts, toasted
1-2 tbsp soy sauce
drizzle of sesame oil

1 Toss the pork in the five-spice powder and season. Heat a wok to very hot, then add the oil. Tip in the pork and cook, stirring, for 2–3 minutes. Add the chilli, half the spring onions, the pepper and veg. Stir-fry for a minute, then add a splash of water and cook for 2 minutes more, until the veg is just tender. Stir in the cashews with the soy sauce and sesame oil to taste.

Serve with rice.

See photo on pages 8–9

Grilled chilli-and-coriander salmon with ginger rice

For perfectly cooked rice every time, bring the water to a hard boil before you add the rice. Keep the water boiling fairly vigorously until the rice is just tender when you bite into a grain. Don't cover the pan, drain the rice as soon as it's ready and serve immediately.

- Serves 2
- Ready in 20 minutes
- Not suitable for freezing

2 tbsp olive oil
1 onion, chopped
small piece of fresh root ginger, finely chopped
1 clove of garlic, thinly sliced
100g basmati rice
2 skinless salmon fillets
1 red chilli, deseeded and finely chopped
small bunch of coriander, chopped

1 Heat 1 tbsp of the oil in a pan and put the kettle on to boil. Fry the onion for a few minutes until lightly browned. Stir in the ginger and garlic, fry for 1 minute, then stir in the rice. Add 300ml boiling water and a little salt, then bring to the boil. Cook for 10 minutes, until the rice is tender. Heat the grill to medium.

2 Lightly brush a baking tray with a little oil. Put the salmon on top and grill for 4–5 minutes, then scatter with the chilli, coriander, remaining olive oil and some seasoning. Grill for 4–5 minutes more, until the salmon is cooked. Serve with the rice.

Serve with lime wedges to squeeze over.

Spicy spaghetti with mushrooms

We've used chestnut mushrooms here because they have a distinctive nutty flavour but button mushrooms would work well too. Instead of a fresh chilli, you could use a sprinkling of dried chilli flakes, if you prefer.

- Serves 4
- Ready in 20 minutes
- Not suitable for freezing

2 tbsp olive oil
250g pack chestnut mushrooms, thickly sliced
1 clove of garlic, thinly sliced
small bunch parsley, leaves only
1 onion, finely chopped
1 celery stick, finely chopped
400g can chopped tomatoes
½ red chilli, deseeded and finely chopped
300g spaghetti

1 Heat 1 tbsp of the oil in a pan, add the mushrooms, then fry over a high heat for 3 minutes until golden and soft. Add the garlic, fry for 1 minute more, then tip into a bowl with the parsley.

2 Put the onion and celery in the pan with the rest of the oil, then fry for 5 minutes. Stir in the tomatoes, chilli and a little salt, then bring to the boil. Reduce the heat and simmer, uncovered, for 10 minutes, until thickened. Meanwhile, boil the spaghetti according to the pack instructions then drain. Toss with the sauce, top with the mushrooms, then serve.

easy
PACKED
LUNCHES
Banish soggy sandwiches for ever!

Bored with the same old lunch every day? Ring the changes with these clever ideas.

If you or your children take your lunch to work or school, now's the time to ditch the usual sandwiches and perk up those lunchboxes. And if you usually head for the sandwich shop at lunchtime, you'll be amazed at how much money you could save if you make something at home instead, even if it's only a few times a week.

You won't find any boring sarnies here – instead of the usual sliced bread, let us tempt you with a range of delicious fillings for tortilla wraps, baguettes and flatbreads. We've come up with ideas that won't turn soggy, and lots of suggestions for alternative fillings. We reckon there are enough recipes in this chapter to keep you going for months!

Fancy something really different? If you have access to a kettle, our *Noodles in a mug* are fab, and if you're really hungry try our hearty *Coronation chicken pasties*, *Meatball and mozzarella calzone* or *Open tuna and sweetcorn melts*. Yum!

Flatbreads filled with halloumi, houmus and salad, page 27

Spicy chicken and bean wrap

If you're eating on the go, cut the wrap into two, wrap with a piece of greaseproof paper and tie with string.

▨ Serves 1
▨ Ready in 5 minutes
▨ Not suitable for freezing

1 large flour tortilla wrap
handful of leftover chicken, shredded
4 tbsp drained black beans or kidney beans
2 tbsp spicy salsa, from a jar
4 slices pickled jalepeño peppers (or a good splash of hot sauce)
3 cherry tomatoes, halved
handful of rocket or spinach leaves

1 Warm the tortilla in the microwave for 10 seconds – this will soften it and make it easier to roll. Put the chicken and beans along the middle and season, then spoon over the salsa and scatter with the peppers or hot sauce. Lay the tomatoes and leaves on top. Bring the bottom of the tortilla up over the filling. Fold the sides in, then roll into a tight wrap.

Alternative ideas
▨ Replace the salsa with guacamole and, for a real kick, use a small, sliced red chilli in place of the jalepeños.
▨ Add a spoonful of soured cream to the wrap before rolling up.

Greek lamb baguette

There's no need to butter the baguette for this – just drizzle with a little olive oil and sprinkle with red wine vinegar for bags of flavour.

▨ Makes 1 (easily multiplied)
▨ Ready in 5 minutes
▨ Not suitable for freezing

1 small baguette, cut lengthways
drizzle of olive oil and sprinkle of red wine vinegar
pinch of dried oregano
handful of leftover roast lamb
few slices of red pepper, deseeded, and red or white onion
handful of shredded lettuce
3 tbsp crumbled feta

1 Sprinkle the inside of the baguette with the olive oil, vinegar, oregano and a little seasoning. Layer the lamb, pepper, onion, lettuce and feta, then serve.

Alternative ideas
▨ This is also delicious made with pastrami in place of the roast lamb.
▨ For a vegetarian version, replace the lamb with extra feta and some sliced olives

Flatbreads filled with halloumi, houmous and salad

Reduced-fat houmous tastes just as good as standard houmous, especially when you're combining it with other ingredients.

- Makes 5
- Ready in 15 minutes
- Not suitable for freezing

pack of 5 Middle Eastern flatbreads
200g tub reduced-fat houmous
250g pack halloumi cheese, sliced
100g bag salad leaves
sliced gherkins, jalapeños and olives
   (optional)

1 Take a flatbread, spread with houmous, then top with a couple of slices of cheese, some salad and the pickles, chillies and olives, if using. Roll up in parchment paper and then a layer of foil.

Alternative ideas
- After spreading with houmous, add baby leaf spinach and some crumbled feta.
- Replace the halloumi and houmous with chopped ham, soft cheese and a little sweet chilli sauce.

See photo on page 24

Open tuna and sweetcorn melts

There's a clever trick here – toast the baguette for a minute of two until it just starts to turn crispy, then when you add the filling the bread won't go soggy. These melts are delicious hot or cold.

- Makes 2
- Ready in 15 minutes
- Not suitable for freezing

1 white or brown sandwich baguette (about
   30cm long)
1 tbsp pesto
80g can tuna, mayonnaise and sweetcorn
   sandwich filling
pinch dried oregano
50g grated cheddar
2 black olives, sliced (optional)

1 Heat the grill to medium, cut the bread in half and flash under the grill for about 30 seconds each side, so the bread dries a little but doesn't turn golden. Spread on the pesto, then spread tuna mix on top. Scatter with the oregano, cheddar and some black pepper. Top each with half olives (if using) and grill until the cheese has melted.

2 Once cool, wrap in parchment paper and foil, or put in an airtight container, then keep chilled until ready to eat.

Alternative ideas
- Replace the sandwich filling with 2 tbsp low-fat soft cheese and some fresh basil leaves.
- Use red leicester cheese in place of the cheddar for extra colour and a milder taste.

Noodles in a mug

You can measure out the liquid ingredients and take them to work in a screwtop jar, pack the veg in a lunchbox and then make up with the noodles in a wide mug at lunchtime.

- Serves 1
- Ready in 10 minutes
- Not suitable for freezing

1 nest fine egg noodles
1 spring onion, finely sliced
3 cherry tomatoes, quartered
1 tbsp passata
1 tsp soy sauce
½ tsp Worcestershire sauce
1 tbsp sweetcorn
1 tsp sesame oil

1 Put the noodles in the bottom of a large mug followed by the spring onions, cherry tomatoes and passata. Pour over enough boiling water to cover then add the rest of the ingredients. Allow to stand for 6 minutes, stirring once.

Alternative ideas
- Add some cooked, finely sliced chicken just before serving.
- Add leftover cooked peas from the night before, either instead of or as well as the sweetcorn.

Salmon and dill pasta salad

Make up a bowl of this salad and store in an airtight container in the fridge for up to 3 days, so you have lunch ready to go each morning.

- Serves 6
- Ready in 20 minutes
- Not suitable for freezing

300g fusilli pasta
213g can wild red salmon
½ cucumber, deseeded and chopped
2 tbsp chopped dill
½ bunch spring onions, sliced
5 tbsp light mayonnaise

1 Cook the pasta according to pack instructions, cool under cold water then drain. Toss with the remaining ingredients (make sure you remove any bones from the salmon) and lots of black pepper.

Alternative ideas
- Use a can of tuna in spring water in place of the red salmon.
- Instead of using fresh dill, use half mayonnaise and half tartare sauce.

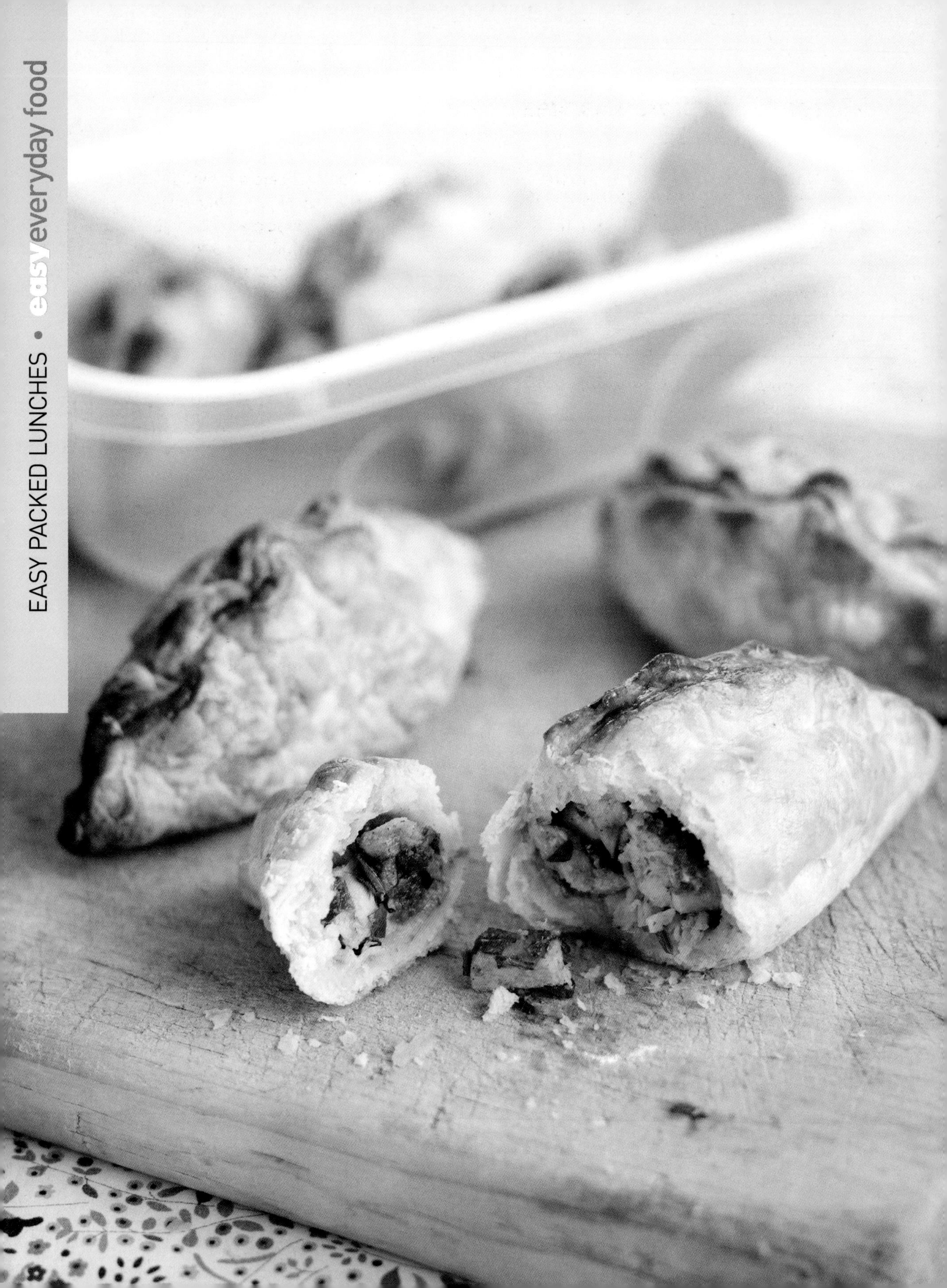

Coronation chicken pasties

Curry powder and crème fraiche make an instant mildly spicy Coronation sauce, and a little mango chutney adds the perfect finishing touch to the filling.

- Makes 10 small pasties
- Takes 50 minutes
- Suitable for freezing (unbaked)

425g pack puff pastry sheets
flour for dusting
2 cooked chicken breasts, chopped (or use
   220g leftover roast chicken)
4 tbsp light crème fraiche
1 tbsp mild curry powder
2 tbsp mango chutney
small bunch chopped coriander
1 egg, beaten

1 Unroll the pastry sheets on a lightly floured surface and cut out 10 circles using a 12cm cutter or a small saucer. Layer up any excess and re-roll. Mix all the remaining ingredients, except the egg, and add a small spoon of filling into the middle of each circle. Brush the edges with egg and bring up the edges to the centre to encase the filling. Press together to seal then crimp with your fingers.

2 Turn the oven to fan 200C/conventional 220C/gas 7. Freeze and chill now or transfer to a baking tray, brush with the egg and bake for 20–25 minutes, until risen and golden. Cool and wrap in cling film or a sandwich bag until ready to eat.

Alternative ideas
- You can fill these with whatever you have left over from dinner the night before: bolognese, curry or casserole (minus most of the gravy) all work well.
- Use cooked roast beef in place of the chicken.

Meatball and mozzarella calzone

These are good hot or cold. To heat them at work, simply microwave for about 2 minutes.

■ Make 12
■ Takes 60 minutes
■ Suitable for freezing (uncooked)

three 145g packs pizza base mix
1-2 tbsp garlic-flavoured olive oil (or use plain olive oil)
350g pack cooked Swedish meatballs, quartered
320g ready-made tomato and basil pasta sauce
220g pack mini mozzarella balls, drained
small bunch basil, chopped

1 Make the dough following packet instructions (if you have a food processor use this and it will be even speedier). Divide the dough into 12 balls and roll out each one to a 20cm circle. Brush with a little of the oil. Mix the remaining ingredients together and then arrange 2-3 tbsp of filling on half of each round, leaving a border, fold over and press to seal, sticking with some more oil.

2 Turn the oven to fan 200C/conventional 220C/gas 8. Brush with more oil (unless freezing now) and pop them on 2 small or 1 large baking tray. Bake for 25 minutes, until golden and risen (or chill and bake just before eating). Delicious hot or cold – to heat simply microwave for about 2 minutes before eating.

Alternative ideas
■ Use chopped cooked sausages in place of the meatballs.
■ Passata works well instead of the ready-made pasta sauce.

Tips for perfect packed lunches

■ In summer, keep a packed lunch cool by freezing a carton of orange juice and popping it into the lunchbox – the juice will have defrosted by lunchtime, ready to drink.

■ Flasks are not just for hot drinks ... In winter, use them to take chunky soup and a hunk of bread or a roll to work.

■ If you have a microwave at work, make the most of it by reheating leftovers from the night before for lunch – keep them chilled until lunchtime, though, and make sure they're piping hot before eating.

■ For kids, cut the bread into fancy shapes with cookie cutters (do a whole loaf at once then put the shapes in the freezer).

■ Keep lunch balanced – include wholegrains (such as wholemeal bread or a handful of mixed seeds), fresh fruit and veg, a protein source and some low-fat dairy.

■ Bite-sized fruit and veg is easier to deal with in a lunchbox than anything you have to peel or cut up, so opt for carrot batons, red pepper slices, cherry tomatoes, tubs of canned fruit in unsweetened juice and dried fruit.

easy
AFTER-SCHOOL SUPPERS
Great ideas for your kids and their friends

Children love bringing their classmates back for tea after school, and these recipes should go down a treat.

Finding something nutritious that they will all enjoy can be a bit of a challenge – even if your own kids are good eaters, you're bound to find that some of their friends are fussy when it comes to food.

The ideas in this chapter are all designed to have mass appeal. Many are classic dishes but with a new and interesting twist; they're all a little out of the ordinary so they feel like a special treat, but they're not so unusual that picky eaters will be reluctant to try them.

If you can, it's a good idea to get the children to help you prepare the meal. Turn it into part of the fun to keep them all occupied and out of trouble and, if they've been involved in putting the dish together, they're far more likely to eat it. They'll love dipping the fish in the breadcrumbs for our *Homemade fish fingers* and being allowed to add toppings to pizza always gets the thumbs up. We've suggested a *Potato and chorizo pizza*, here, but you can use the tortilla base for any other toppings that they fancy.

Easy cheese jackets, page 38

Oven-baked egg and chips

An easy twist on a classic supper dish. If you like, you can add a few button mushrooms in with the tomatoes and roll up some streaky bacon rashers to cook with the potatoes for the last 6–8 minutes.

▨ Serves 2
▨ Ready in 35 minutes
▨ Not suitable for freezing

2 medium baking potatoes, cut into chunky wedges
2 tbsp olive oil
1 tsp smoked paprika
2 tomatoes, halved
2 eggs

1 Turn the oven to fan 170C/conventional 190C/gas 5. Tip the potato wedges into a roasting tin. Drizzle over the oil and sprinkle over the paprika. Season and mix well to coat the potatoes. Roast for 25 minutes, turning halfway through, until almost tender.

2 Put the tomatoes, cut-side up, among the potatoes. Make 2 spaces in the tin and crack an egg into each one. Return to the oven for 6–8 minutes until the eggs are just set.

Cheesy broccoli pasta

This is so easy, it's bound to become one of your weeknight regulars and it's a great way of smuggling some veg into kids' meals. Wholegrain mustard is very mild, so don't be tempted to leave it out.

▨ Serves 4
▨ Ready in 30 minutes
▨ Not suitable for freezing

280g penne
280g broccoli, cut into florets
25g butter
25g plain flour
300ml milk
1 tbsp wholegrain mustard
140g mature cheddar, grated

1 Cook the pasta according to pack instructions, adding the broccoli for the final 4–5 minutes and cooking until tender. Drain well, then heat the grill.

2 Heat the butter in a pan and stir in the flour. Cook for 1 minute, then gradually add the milk, stirring well between each addition. Bring to the boil, stirring, then simmer for 2 minutes, before mixing in the mustard, half the cheese and some seasoning.

3 Mix the pasta and broccoli into the sauce and spoon into an ovenproof dish. Scatter over the remaining cheese and put under a hot grill for 3–4 minutes, until golden and bubbling.

Easy cheese jackets

Jacket potatoes usually take too long to cook for an after-school supper, but if you microwave them, add a filling and then crisp them up under a hot grill at the end – it speeds things up beautifully. Use double Gloucester cheese to add extra colour too.

▦ Serves 2
▦ Ready in 25 minutes
▦ Not suitable for freezing

2 large baking potatoes
50g butter
100g double gloucester cheese, chopped
1 tbsp fresh, snipped chives
50g mushrooms, chopped

1 Prick each potato in several places with a fork. Stand on a double thickness of kitchen paper and cook on full power (100%) for 12–13 minutes, until tender.

2 Halve each potato and scoop out the flesh with a spoon, leaving a little inside the skins to help them stand up. Mix the butter, cheese, chives and mushrooms into the potato flesh, season and pile back into the skins. Put on a microwaveable flan dish and cook on medium power (50%). Finish for a few minutes under a hot grill.

Serve with salad.

See photo on page 34

Chipolata and spring onion frittata

These quantities serve 4, but they're easy to scale down if you're just feeding two children. The bread helps the frittata to set nicely and gives it a lovely texture.

▦ Serves 4
▦ Ready in 25 minutes
▦ Not suitable for freezing

1 tbsp olive oil
340g pack chipolatas
6 eggs
2 slices bread, about 50g, torn into small pieces
1 bunch spring onions, thinly sliced
2 cloves of garlic, finely chopped

1 Heat the oil in a 20cm non-stick frying pan. Add the chipolatas and cook for 7–8 minutes, until browned. Meanwhile, crack the eggs into a large bowl and beat well. Stir in the bread, spring onions and garlic with some salt and pepper.

2 Heat the grill to medium. Pour the egg mixture into the hot pan and cook on the lowest heat for about 6–7 minutes, until the egg is almost completely set. Put the pan under the grill for 2–3 minutes, until golden brown and cooked through.

Serve with baked beans or salad, if you like.

Crisp parmesan chicken with broccoli

Use chicken thighs rather than breasts for this as they have more flavour and they're cheaper too! If your children aren't keen on broccoli, use another green veg instead (although if you steam the broccoli rather then boiling it, you may find they're happy to tuck in).

- Serves 2
- Ready in 50 minutes
- Not suitable for freezing

4 skinless, boneless chicken thighs
50g parmesan, finely grated
50g white breadcrumbs
1 tbsp flour
1 egg, beaten
1 small broccoli head, broken into florets
25g butter
1 clove of garlic, sliced
grated rind and juice of ½ lemon

1 Turn the oven to fan 180C/conventional 200C/gas 6. Season the chicken thighs. Mix the parmesan and breadcrumbs on 1 plate and put the flour and beaten egg onto 2 more separate plates. Coat each chicken thigh in the flour first, dusting off the excess, then dip in the egg and then roll in the breadcrumbs. Sit on a rack over a baking tray and bake for 40 minutes, until crisp and golden.

2 Boil or steam the broccoli until tender, then drain. Melt the butter in a pan and gently sizzle the garlic for 2–3 minutes. Add the lemon rind and juice and season. Toss with the broccoli and serve with the chicken.

Spicy meatballs

Turkey mince is very good value and makes excellent meatballs. These freeze well, so why not make a big batch so you've got some ready for another time as well?

- Serves 6
- Ready in 35 minutes
- Suitable for freezing

500g turkey mince
1 onion, chopped
2 cloves of garlic, chopped
2 tsp mild curry powder
2 tsp ground cumin
1 tsp garam masala
½ tsp paprika or cayenne pepper
2 tbsp fresh coriander, chopped
1 egg, beaten
50g fresh breadcrumbs
1 tbsp oil

1 Turn the oven to fan 160C/conventional 180C/gas 4. Put the mince into a mixing bowl. Add the onion, garlic, curry powder, cumin, garam masala, paprika or cayenne pepper and coriander, then mix well. Add the beaten egg and breadcrumbs, then mix again. Divide the mixture into 15–18 evenly-sized pieces and shape into balls (they should be about the size of a walnut).

2 Heat the oil in a frying pan over a medium heat and cook the meatballs for 5 minutes, turning until golden brown. Remove from the pan and put them on a baking tray. Bake in the oven for 15–20 minutes. Remove from the oven and leave to cool.

Serve with a green salad, some pitta bread and a pot of tomato ketchup or tomato salsa on the side.

Tasty chicken noodles

Use fish sauce if you've already got a bottle but, if not, soy sauce makes a good substitute. For extra crunch, add a handful of cashews with the chicken and spices in step 2.

- Serves 2 (easily doubled)
- Ready in 15 minutes
- Not suitable for freezing

2 tsp cornflour
2 tbsp fish sauce or soy sauce
1 tbsp caster sugar
2 blocks medium egg noodles
1 tbsp sunflower oil
1 large red pepper, deseeded and chopped
2 cloves of garlic, thinly sliced
4 spring onions, sliced
200g leftover roast chicken, shredded
1 tsp ground coriander
½ tsp chilli powder
100g frozen peas
10g basil or coriander, leaves roughly shredded

1 Mix the cornflour with the fish or soy sauce and sugar, then gradually add 8 tbsp water and mix until smooth. Cook the noodles in boiling water for 4 minutes.

2 Meanwhile, heat the oil in a wok, then stir-fry the pepper, garlic and spring onions for about 3 minutes. Tip in the chicken, spices and peas, stir-fry for a couple of seconds more, then pour in the fish sauce and flour mixture. Stir until thickened, then toss in the drained noodles and basil or coriander.

Homemade fish fingers

Fish fingers are surprisingly easy to make and much tastier than anything you can buy in the shops. Kids will enjoy helping you roll them in the breadcrumbs before you bake them – though things may get a little messy!

- Serves 4
- Ready in 30 minutes
- Suitable for freezing (uncooked)

1 egg, beaten
85g white breadcrumbs, made from day-old bread
1 lemon, grated rind and juice
1 tsp dried oregano
1 tbsp olive oil
400g skinless white fish, such as pollack, sliced into 12 strips
4 tbsp mayonnaise
140g frozen peas, cooked and cooled
100g baby leaf spinach

1 Turn the oven to fan 180C/conventional 200C/gas 6. Pour the beaten egg into a shallow dish. Tip the breadcrumbs onto a plate. Mix in the lemon rind, oregano and salt and pepper.

2 Brush a non-stick baking sheet with half the oil. Dip the fish strips into the egg, then roll them in the breadcrumbs. Transfer to the baking sheet and bake for 20 minutes, until golden and cooked through.

3 Meanwhile, mix the mayo with a squeeze of lemon juice. Toss the peas and spinach leaves with a squeeze more lemon juice and the remaining oil. Serve the fish fingers with the veg and a spoonful of the lemon-mayo.

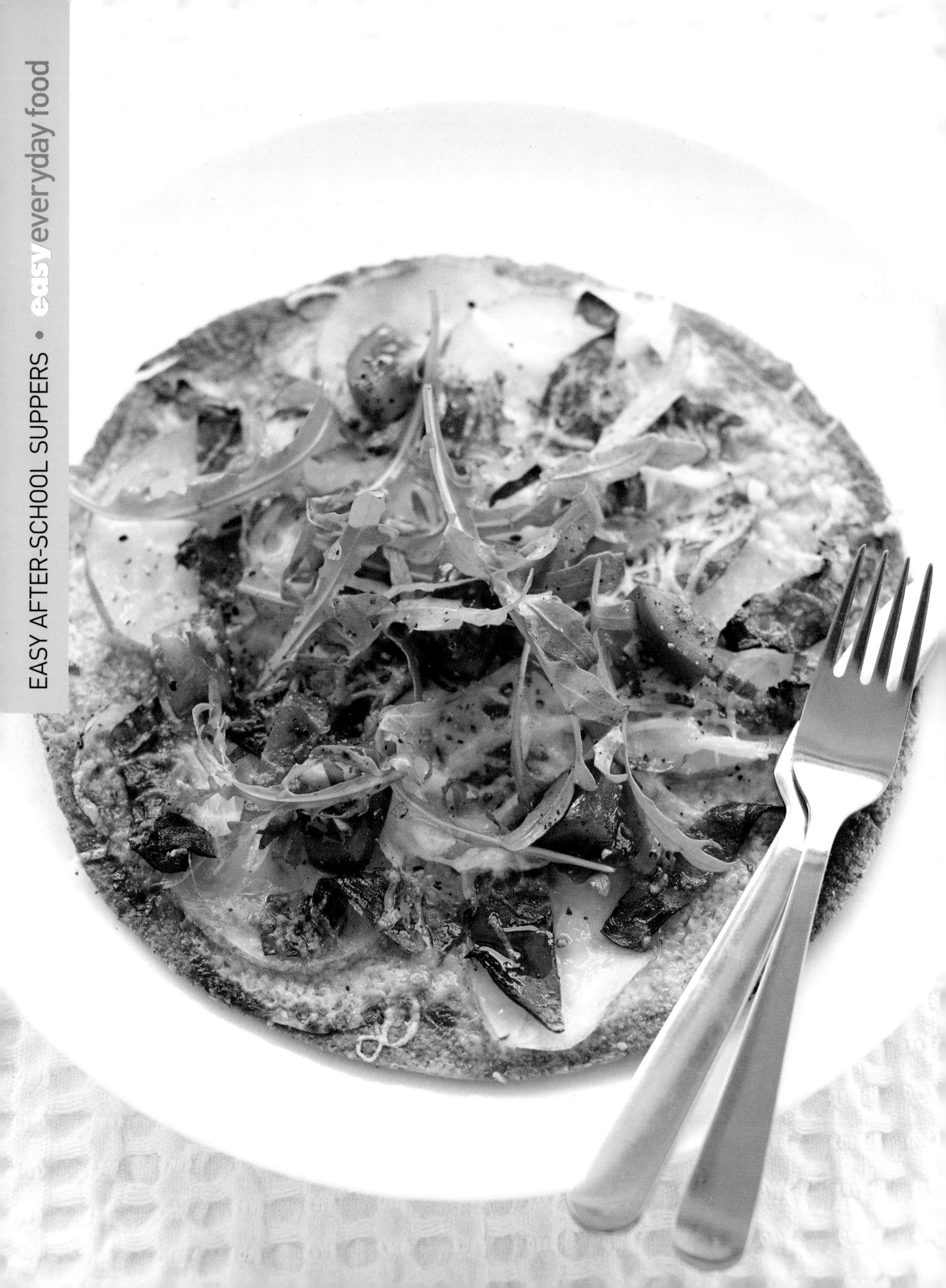

Potato and chorizo pizza with tomato salad

You can use any combinations of your favourite pizza toppings on this quick tortilla base, and although the salad looks good piled on top, you can serve it on the side (or replace it with veg), if you prefer.

- Serves 4
- Ready in 20 minutes
- Not suitable for freezing

3 medium potatoes, very thinly sliced
4 wholemeal tortillas
6 tbsp half-fat crème fraiche
½ onion, thinly sliced
8 thin slices chorizo from a pack, diced
25g mature cheddar, grated
3 tomatoes, roughly chopped
2 tsp balsamic dressing
25g rocket

1 Turn the oven to fan 180C/conventional 200C/gas 6. Bring a pan of water to the boil, then blanch the potato slices for 2 minutes, or until almost cooked. Drain well, then tip onto kitchen paper to dry.

2 Put the tortillas onto baking sheets. Season the crème fraiche, then spread over the tortillas. Top with the cooked potato slices, onion and chorizo, then scatter over the grated cheese. Bake for 8 minutes, until crisp and golden.

3 Meanwhile, mix the tomatoes with the dressing and ½ tsp coarsely ground black pepper, then toss through the rocket. Pile a quarter of the salad in the middle of each tortilla and serve.

Sweetcorn and tuna bake

Tube-style pasta shapes work best in bakes like this. We've used rigatoni, but penne or macaroni would be good too.

- Serves 6
- Ready in 35 minutes
- Not suitable for freezing

600g rigatoni
50g butter
50g plain flour
600ml milk
250g mature cheddar, grated
two 160g cans tuna steaks in spring water, drained
340g can sweetcorn, drained
large handful of chopped parsley

1 Turn the oven to fan 160C/conventional 180C/gas 4. Boil the pasta for 2 minutes less time than stated in pack instructions.

2 Melt the butter in a pan and stir in the flour. Cook for 1 minute, then gradually stir in the milk to make a thick white sauce. Remove from the heat and stir in all but a handful of the cheese.

3 Drain the pasta, mix with the white sauce, tuna, sweetcorn and parsley, then season. Transfer to a baking dish and top with the rest of the grated cheese. Bake for 15–20 minutes, until the cheese on top is golden and starting to brown.

Serve with a green salad.

easy
FAMILY FAVOURITES
Delicious meals you can enjoy together

Sitting down and eating as a family can bring so many rewards, and everyone will love these yummy recipes.

We all lead such busy live these days and it's easy for a family to become like ships that pass in the night, all rushing off in different directions with barely time to exchange a few words. But it's worth making time to sit down at the table as often as possible to enjoy a meal together. It's often said that 'the family who eats together, stays together' and that's so true, especially if there are teenagers around. It's amazing how much easier it is to discuss tricky topics when you've all got a meal to focus on, and all sorts of things might come out casually in conversation over the dinner table that you'd never otherwise have found out about.

It's also the only way that younger children can learn good table manners, and it will encourage them to try new foods if they see the rest of the family tucking in (both of which will stand them in very good stead for later life).

So, cook up one of the meals on the following pages and you can be sure that the delicious aromas wafting from the kitchen will have them all flocking to the table.

One-pan chicken couscous, page 50

Easy chicken pie

Condensed soup makes a brilliant quick-and-easy sauce. If you don't have any sweetcorn you can use 250g cooked peas and you can leave out the crème fraiche and use a knob of butter instead, if you prefer.

- Serves 4
- Ready in 45 minutes
- Suitable for freezing

1 onion, sliced
400g pack skinless chicken thighs, cut into chunks
1 tbsp vegetable oil
250ml chicken stock
325g can sweetcorn, drained
295g can condensed cream of mushroom soup
handful of parsley or basil leaves, chopped
750g potatoes, cut into chunks
3 tbsp half-fat crème fraiche

1 Fry the onion and chicken in the oil for 5–10 minutes, until the onion is soft and the chicken is golden. Pour over the stock, bring to the boil, then simmer for 20 minutes until the chicken is cooked. Stir in the corn, the condensed soup and the herbs. Season and warm through.

2 Meanwhile, boil the potatoes until soft. Drain and mash with the crème fraiche and some seasoning. Spoon the chicken mix into 4 pie dishes and top with the mash. Put on a baking tray, then grill until the potato is golden.

Classic spaghetti carbonara

So easy, and so delicious! For an authentic carbonara there should be enough sauce to coat the pasta, but it shouldn't be swimming in it. Smoked back bacon is usually cut more thinly than pancetta, but the flavour of both is very similar.

- Serves 6
- Ready in 20 minutes
- Not suitable for freezing

600g spaghetti
300g smoked back bacon or pancetta, cut into thin strips
4 eggs
100ml single cream
100g grated parmesan, plus extra to serve
handful of flat-leaf parsley, chopped

1 Cook the pasta according to pack instructions. Meanwhile, heat a large, non-stick frying pan and dry-fry the bacon or pancetta for 3 minutes, stirring often, until crisp. Crack the eggs into a bowl and mix lightly with a fork, but don't scramble them. Stir in the cream, a little salt and lots of black pepper.

2 Drain the pasta, reserving a little of the cooking water. Return to the pan over a low heat and add the bacon or pancetta. Toss well and cook for a minute, then add the egg mixture and the parmesan, and cook for 30 seconds more, or until the egg is just setting. Add the chopped parsley and serve immediately.

Serve with extra parmesan, if you like, and a good grating of freshly ground black pepper.

One-pan chicken couscous

Meals that can be cooked in one pan make life so easy, not least because they save on washing up! The dried apricots add a lovely sweetness to the recipe, while harissa (a hot chilli paste) gives it a bit of a kick.

▦ Serves 4
▦ Ready in 15 minutes
▦ Not suitable for freezing

1 tbsp olive oil
1 onion, thinly sliced
200g chicken breast, diced
good chunk of fresh root ginger
1–2 tbsp harissa paste
10 dried apricots
220g can chickpeas, rinsed and drained
200g couscous
200ml hot chicken stock
handful of coriander, chopped, to garnish

1 Heat the olive oil in a large frying pan and cook the onion for 1–2 minutes, until just softened. Add the chicken and fry for 7–10 minutes, until cooked through and the onions have turned golden. Grate over the ginger, stir through the harissa to coat everything and cook for 1 minute more.

2 Tip in the apricots, chickpeas and couscous, then pour over the stock and stir once. Cover with a lid and leave for about 5 minutes until the couscous has soaked up all the stock and is soft. Fluff up the couscous with a fork and scatter over the coriander to serve.

See photo on page 46

Macaroni cheese with bacon

This is a classic comfort food dish, and using vibrant red leicester cheese and adding some chopped bacon gives it a new twist. Don't be tempted to leave out the mustard powder as it really brings out the subtle flavour of the cheese.

▦ Serves 2
▦ Ready in 40 minutes
▦ Not suitable for freezing

1 handful of chunky breadcrumbs
drizzle of olive oil
1 tbsp butter
1 clove of garlic, finely chopped
1 tsp mustard powder
1 tbsp flour
250ml whole milk
100g red leicester, grated
175g rigatoni or penne
4 slices streaky bacon, grilled until crisp

1 Turn the oven to fan 180C/conventional 200C/gas 6. Put the breadcrumbs on a baking sheet, drizzle with the oil, season with salt and ground black pepper and bake for 5 minutes.

2 Melt the butter in a pan. Add the garlic and mustard, and cook for 1 minute. Add the flour and whisk on a low heat for 1 minute. Gradually whisk in the milk, then bring to a boil, continuing to whisk. Reduce the heat and simmer until thick (about 4 minutes). Stir in the cheese until melted.

3 Meanwhile, cook the pasta in boiling water according to pack instructions, then drain and mix with the cheese sauce and bacon. Spoon into 2 large ramekins, top with breadcrumbs and bake for 20 minutes, until golden.

Mustard toad in the hole

You can either make one big toad, as here, or try these mini toads: put ½ tsp sunflower oil in each cup of a 12-hole mini muffin pan, set on a baking tray. Turn the oven to fan 180C/conventional 200C/gas 6. Heat the pan in the oven until the oil is hot. Whisk 85ml milk, 1 egg, 50g plain flour and a pinch of salt to make a batter and fill the cups to just under two-thirds full. Add 1 cocktail sausage to each and bake for 25 minutes.

- Serves 4
- Ready in 1 hour 5 minutes
- Not suitable for freezing

8 pork sausages
2 onions, cut into wedges
2 tbsp olive oil
150g plain flour
2 tsp English mustard powder
2 eggs
300ml milk

1 Turn the oven to fan 180C/conventional 200C/gas 6. Put the sausages and onions in an ovenproof baking dish. Drizzle over the oil, season, then cook for 20 minutes until everything is lightly browned.

2 Meanwhile, put the flour and mustard powder into a bowl and season. Gradually whisk in the eggs and milk to make a batter. Pour into the hot dish with the sausages, then cook for 35 minutes more, until crisp and golden.

Fastest-ever beef stew

It's not usually possible to make a stew like this in the microwave because the fast cooking time leaves the meat rather tough. But if you use feather steak and add it right at the end, it cooks quickly and stays wonderfully moist and tender.

- Serves 4
- Ready in 25 minutes
- Not suitable for freezing

100g carrots, chopped
100g courgettes, chopped
1 onion, chopped
1 tsp dried mixed herbs
200g potatoes, peeled and chopped
300ml beef stock
150ml red wine
1 tbsp tomato ketchup
2 tbsp cornflour, blended with a little water
300g feather steak, trimmed and cut into 5cm slices

1 Put all the ingredients except the beef into a 2.5-litre microwaveable casserole dish, cover with cling film and make 2 slits in it to allow the steam to escape. Cook on full power (100%) for 13 minutes, stirring once. Add the beef and cook on full power (100%) for a further 3 minutes, or until the vegetables are tender, then allow to stand for 5 minutes before serving.

Serve with mash or boiled potatoes.

Oat-topped fish pie

Instead of a pastry lid for this pie, we've combined flour, rolled oats and butter to make a topping that's a bit like a savoury crumble. And, unlike shortcrust pastry, there's no fiddly 'rubbing in' required – you just need to mash in the butter with a fork.

▨ Serves 6
▨ Ready in 45 minutes
▨ Not suitable for freezing

250g plain flour
50g rolled oats
150g cold butter, chopped into small pieces
50g hard cheese (such as cheddar), grated
500g skinless and boneless cod fillets
2 large carrots
100g frozen peas
400g large, cooked and peeled prawns (thawed if frozen)
450ml milk
30g chopped parsley
1 bay leaf

1 Turn the oven to fan 180C/conventional 200C/gas 6. Put 200g of flour and the oats into a bowl. Add 100g of the butter, then mash it into the flour and oat mixture with a fork, until it resembles large breadcrumbs. Mix in the cheese.

2 Cut the cod and carrots into finger-sized pieces and put into a shallow, buttered ovenproof dish with the peas and prawns.

3 Melt the remaining butter over a medium heat. Remove the pan from the heat, then add the remaining 50g flour, stirring to form a thick, smooth paste. Put the pan back on the heat and cook for 2 minutes. Gradually add the milk, a little at a time, and stir with a wooden spoon, making sure that no lumps appear, until you have a smooth sauce. This mixture should be the consistency of double cream. Simmer for 2 minutes and season.

4 Add the parsley and bay leaf to the sauce, then pour over the fish, carrots, peas and prawns. Sprinkle the cheesy oat mixture over the sauce. Bake for approximately 20–25 minutes, or until the topping is golden and crunchy.

Serve with a crispy salad or mashed root vegetables, such as potatoes and carrots.

Sausages with sweet potato mash

Sweet potatoes make really good mash for a change, and chipolatas are quicker to cook than ordinary sausages. You can speed things up even more by microwaving the sweet potatoes – peel them, cut into equal-sized chunks, cover tightly with cling film and pierce the film once. Microwave on full power (100%) for 5 minutes.

▓ Serves 2 (easily multiplied)
▓ Ready in 30 minutes
▓ Not suitable for freezing

6 chipolata sausages
1 small onion, sliced
400g can chopped tomatoes
small handful of sage leaves, chopped
3 sweet potatoes, peeled and cut into chunks
drizzle of olive oil

1 Heat the grill. Put the sausages in a shallow ovenproof dish with the onion and grill for 10 minutes, turning the sausages occasionally. Add the tomatoes and sage. Season and stir well. Grill again for 10 minutes, or until the tomatoes start to brown around the edges.

2 Meanwhile, boil the sweet potatoes until just tender, about 7–8 minutes, then roughly crush with a little olive oil and seasoning. Serve with the sausages.

Pesto and salami puff pizza

Pesto and salami are an unusual flavour combination, but they taste great together – and a sheet of ready-made puff pastry makes a great pizza base (though you can use pizza dough, if you prefer – make it up and cook according to the directions on the pack).

▓ Serves 4
▓ Ready in 25 minutes
▓ Not suitable for freezing

375g sheet ready-rolled puff pastry
5 tbsp red pesto
70g pack sliced salami
125g ball mozzarella, torn into pieces

1 Turn the oven to fan 200C/conventional 220C/gas 7. Unroll the pastry onto a large baking sheet and prick all over with a fork. Spread over the pesto, leaving a border of roughly 2cm around the edge. Layer on the salami, top with the torn mozzarella and some seasoning, then bake for 15–20 minutes, until the pastry is golden, risen and crisp.

Serve drizzled with a little olive oil and scattered with a few rocket leaves.

easy
FRIDAY NIGHT TAKEAWAYS
Don't dial out for one – make your own!

We all love Friday nights: the working week is over, the weekend is stretching ahead of us and it's time to kick back and relax.

But instead of reaching for the takeaway menu this friday, how about cooking your own delicious version of one of your favourites? It's likely to be a lot healthier than your usual takeaway meal, you'll know exactly what's gone into it and it'll save you money too. It's a win-win situation!

If Chinese is the takeaway you like best, try our *Chicken in peanut sauce* and *Egg fried rice with prawns and peas* or one of our lovely stir-fries (you'll find some useful tips for cooking the perfect stir-fry on page 59).

Prefer Indian food? Takeaway kormas are delicious but they can be really high in fat and calories. Our *Low-cal chicken korma*, on the other hand, comes in at just 400 kcals and 3g saturated fat per portion.

There's also a fantastic pizza that uses ricotta instead of the more usual mozzarella for the topping, plus a healthy twist on fish and chips and three gorgeous recipes inspired by American diner-style takeouts.

Ham and ricotta pizza, page 69

Chicken in peanut sauce

This can be ready and on the table in just 15 minutes. But if you have time in the morning, get it ready up to the end of step 1, cover and leave the chicken to marinate in the fridge for even more flavour.

- Serves 2
- Ready in 15 minutes
- Not suitable for freezing

2 chicken breasts, cut into chunks
2 tbsp coconut cream
1½ tbsp lemon juice
1 tbsp soy sauce
pinch of chilli powder
1 tbsp vegetable oil
1 clove of garlic, crushed
½ tsp each ground turmeric, five-spice powder, coriander seeds and cumin seeds
2 tbsp peanut butter

1 Put the chicken in a microwaveable flan dish with all the other ingredients, except the peanut butter and ½ tbsp of the lemon juice.

2 Cover the chicken dish with clingfilm, pierce a few holes in it and cook on full power (100%) for 6–8 minutes, until the chicken is cooked through, stirring once.

3 Stir the remaining ½ tbsp lemon juice into the peanut butter to loosen it a little, then stir into the chicken. Leave to stand for 2 minutes before serving.

Serve with rice, with baby leaf spinach leaves stirred through (which will wilt in the heat, so no need to cook the spinach first).

Stir-fried spicy beef with rice and greens

Use scissors to cut the steak into thin strips – you'll find it's much easier than cutting it with a knife. When they're in season, spring greens are ideal for this recipe but shredded cabbage works really well too. We've used brown basmati rice here, for its deliciously nutty taste. The recipe is good with strips of chicken or pork too.

- Serves 2
- Ready in 15 minutes
- Not suitable for freezing

250g lean sirloin or frying steak, trimmed of all fat and cut into thin strips
1 tbsp sunflower oil
thumb-sized piece root ginger, shredded
2 tsp Chinese five-spice powder
200g spring greens, shredded
1 tbsp soy sauce
1 pack brown basmati rice, heated according to pack instructions
4 spring onions, shredded
1 red chilli, deseeded and shredded

1 Stir-fry the beef in the oil until browned, then add the ginger and fry for 1 minute more. Add the five-spice powder, cook for another minute, then add the greens with a splash of water and the soy sauce, and stir-fry until just tender. Add the rice and toss everything together. Serve topped with the spring onions and chilli.

Tips for a speedy stir-fry

■ Prepare all the ingredients before you start cooking.

■ Unless otherwise stated, cut all the ingredients into similar-sized pieces.

■ Move the ingredients continually around the hot wok or frying pan, so that they cook evenly and don't burn. Add a splash of water to stop foods sticking and to create steam, which will help them to cook.

■ Look out for big packs of stir-fry veg from the supermarket – they're really good value and save a lot of preparation time.

Egg-fried rice with prawns and peas

Express rice pouches make life so easy – they're quick to use and there's no washing up involved! There's no need to defrost the peas first as they will quickly cook in the heat of the pan and if you like spicy food, leave the seeds in the chilli.

▨ Serves 4
▨ Ready in 20 minutes
▨ Not suitable for freezing

two 250g pouches express rice
2 tbsp vegetable oil
2 cloves of garlic, finely chopped
1 red chilli, deseeded and shredded
2 eggs, beaten
200g frozen peas
1 bunch spring onions, finely sliced
285g pack small, cooked and peeled prawns
1 tbsp soy sauce

1 Cook the rice according to pack instructions. Heat the oil in a wok or large frying pan. Add the garlic and chilli, then cook for 10 seconds, stirring constantly. Add the cooked rice, stir-fry for 1 minute, then push to the side of the pan.

2 Pour the eggs into the empty side of the pan, then scramble them, stirring. Once they're just set, stir the peas and spring onions into the rice, stir in the egg, then cook for 2 minutes until the peas are tender. Add the prawns and soy sauce, then heat through.

Aubergine and black bean stir fry

Not all brands of black bean sauce are vegetarian, so check the label if you're making this for a non meat-eater. Basmati rice works best with this recipe because of its subtly perfumed flavour but long grain rice is fine to use instead (look out for packs labelled 'easy cook' rice as they cook more quickly).

▨ Serves 4
▨ Ready in 30 minutes
▨ Not suitable for freezing

250g basmati rice
4 tbsp vegetable oil
2 large aubergines, cut into quarters and then wedges
2 red peppers, deseeded and cut into thin strips
8 spring onions, 7 quartered lengthways, 1 finely sliced
220g jar black bean sauce

1 Cook the rice according to pack instructions. Meanwhile, heat a wok and add the oil. When hot, stir-fry the aubergines for 10–12 minutes until golden and cooked through. Add the peppers and the quartered spring onions, and stir-fry for about 6 minutes until just tender.

2 Add the black bean sauce and 2 tbsp water, and warm through. Serve with the basmati rice, scattered with the finely sliced spring onion.

Low-cal chicken korma

All the taste but fewer calories – this has just 400 kcals a portion and 3g of saturated fat. Bring the yogurt to room temperature before you use it and add it slowly a little at a time, or it may curdle the sauce.

- Serves 4
- Ready in 50 minutes
- Not suitable for freezing

2 tbsp vegetable oil
2 medium onions, chopped
3 garlic cloves
2 tbsp chopped ginger
5 cardamom pods
1 cinnamon stick
600g skinless chicken breasts, cut into bite-sized pieces
2 tsp ground coriander
1½ tsp garam masala
¼ tsp ground mace
¼ tsp ground black pepper
150g natural yogurt, not fridge-cold
100ml whole milk
2 small green chillies, deseeded and shredded

1 Heat 1 tbsp of the oil in a deep pan. Tip in the onions and cook for 12–15 minutes, stirring occasionally, until golden. Remove from the heat. Transfer a third of the mixture to a small blender along with the garlic, ginger and 2 tbsp water. Whizz together to make a paste. Set aside.

2 Return the onions in the pan to the heat, add the remaining oil, cardamom pods and cinnamon stick, then stir-fry for 2–3 minutes. Stir in the chicken, ground coriander, garam masala, mace and black pepper, then stir-fry for 2 minutes more. Reserve 3 tbsp of the yogurt, then slowly add the rest, 1 tbsp at a time, stirring between each spoonful, then add the paste and cook for 2–3 minutes more.

3 Stir in 150ml water and the milk. Bring to a boil, then simmer, covered, for 20 minutes or until the chicken is tender, adding the chillies for the final 5 minutes. Remove the cardamom pods and cinnamon pods.

Serve with rice, a spoonful of yogurt and a few flaked almonds and coriander leaves, if you like.

Aubergine and mushroom curry

Wash your hands in cold water when you've chopped chillies and onions, to get rid of the smell.

▨ Serves 4
▨ Ready in 30 minutes
▨ Not suitable for freezing

2 aubergines, each cut into about 8 chunks
3 tbsp olive oil
250g chestnut mushrooms, halved
20g bunch coriander, stalks and leaves separated
2 large onions, roughly chopped
thumb-size piece of fresh root ginger
3 cloves of garlic, coarsely chopped
1 fat red chilli, deseeded, half roughly chopped and half thinly shredded
1 tbsp each ground cumin and ground coriander
1 tbsp tomato purée
500ml vegetable stock
5 tbsp ground almonds
200g natural full-fat yogurt

1 Fry the aubergine chunks in 2 tbsp of the oil for about 10 minutes, until golden brown and soft. Add the mushrooms after 5 minutes, fry until golden, then tip out of the pan. Meanwhile, whizz the coriander stalks, onions, ginger, garlic and chopped chilli to a paste in a food processor. Add another tbsp of oil to the pan, then fry the paste for 3 minutes, until soft.

2 Tip in the spices and tomato purée. Stir for 2 minutes more, then return the aubergines and mushrooms to the pan. Tip in the stock, ground almonds and most of the yogurt. Simmer for 5 minutes, until the sauce has thickened a little. Scatter the shredded chilli over the curry with the chopped coriander leaves. Drizzle over the remaining yogurt to serve.

Coconut dhal

This makes a great side dish, or serve it with a spoonful of mango chutney and plenty of naan bread as a main course. Larger supermarkets now stock dried curry leaves, so use them if you can find them as they add an authentic flavour – if not, coriander leaves are a good alternative.

▨ Serves 4
▨ Ready in 25 minutes
▨ Suitable for freezing

250g red lentils
400ml can coconut milk
2 onions, 1 chopped and 1 sliced
2 medium tomatoes, chopped
2–3 green chillies, sliced
1 tsp turmeric
4 tbsp olive oil
handful of curry leaves or coriander leaves
2 tsp mustard seeds

1 Put the lentils, coconut milk, the chopped onion, tomatoes, chillies and turmeric in a pan with 300ml water. Season, and then simmer for 20 minutes until the lentils are tender.

2 Meanwhile, fry the sliced onion in the oil until crisp, add the curry or coriander leaves and mustard seeds, and cook for a few seconds.

Serve with the crispy onions on top.

Black bean curry

Look out for jars of smoky pimentón – the Spanish version of paprika – in the herbs and spices aisle of the supermarket (or use mild chilli powder instead, if you can't find any).

- Serves 4–6
- Ready in 30 minutes
- Suitable for freezing

2 tbsp olive oil
4 cloves of garlic, finely chopped
2 large onions, chopped
3 tbsp sweet pimentón
3 tbsp ground cumin
3 tbsp cider vinegar
2 tbsp brown sugar
two 400g cans chopped tomatoes
two 400g cans black beans, rinsed and drained

1 In a large pan, heat the olive oil and fry the garlic and onions for 5 minutes, until almost softened. Add the pimentón or chilli powder and cumin, cook for a few minutes, then add the vinegar, sugar, tomatoes and some seasoning. Cook for 10 minutes. Tip in the beans and cook for another 10 minutes.

Serve with rice and side dishes, such as crumbled feta, chopped spring onions, sliced avocado, sliced radishes and soured cream.

Barbecued corn with summery butter

The flavoured butter is great melted onto steaks too. You can grill the cobs instead of barbecuing them – preheat the grill to medium and cook the cobs for 15–20 minutes, turning occasionally.

- Serves 4
- Ready in 30 minutes
- Suitable for freezing (flavoured butter only)

15g pack coriander
100g soft butter
grated rind of 1 lime and juice of ½
4 fresh corn cobs, with husks attached

1 Turn the oven to fan 200C/conventional 220C/gas 7. Strip the leaves from the coriander and put in a mini food processor with the butter, a little salt, and the lime rind and juice. Pulse until well blended. (If you don't have a small processor, finely chop the coriander and fold into the butter along with the lime rind and juice.) Roll the mixture into a log shape, wrap in cling film and chill until needed.

2 Meanwhile, peel the husks of the corn back, but leave them attached. Remove the silk and rinse well to remove remaining silk strands. Smooth the husks back over the cobs. Don't worry if some of the cobs are partially exposed. Wrap the corn cobs in foil if you can't find cobs with husks.

3 Put over medium-hot coals for 20 minutes, or until tender. Slice the coriander butter into cylinders. Peel away the husks of the corn and serve with the butter slices on top and a couple of extra lime wedges, if you like.

Jerk-spiced ribs

The ribs are braised first and then they're finished off on the barbecue – or you can finish off in the oven at fan 180C/conventional 200C/gas 6 instead. Roast for 30 minutes or until browned.

- Serves 8
- Ready in 1 hour
- Not suitable for freezing

1 bunch spring onions
1 tsp allspice berries
2 baby rack of ribs or 2kg ready-cut ribs
1 chicken stock cube
3 red chillies, deseeded and chopped
3 cloves of garlic, chopped
small piece of root ginger, chopped
juice of 2 limes
6 sprigs thyme, leaves removed and chopped
small bunch of coriander, chopped
1 tsp cinnamon
1 tsp ground cloves
3 tbsp dark brown sugar
4 tbsp vegetable oil

1 Turn the oven to fan 140C/conventional 160C/gas 3. Chop the dark green of the spring onions and put in a large roasting tin with the allspice. Add the rib racks and boiling water to cover. Add the stock cube, cover with foil and cook for 2 hours.

2 Drain off the cooking liquid. Chop the rest of the spring onions and put in a food processor with the rest of the ingredients and half a mug of water. Whizz to make a marinade. Rub the racks. Leave for 30 minutes.

3 Cook on the BBQ for about 20 minutes until browned but not blackened, turning them often to stop them from burning. Leave to rest for 10 minutes before carving.

Really easy beefburgers

There's a secret weapon in this recipe – rather than chopping up lots of ingredients to add to the mince, just a teaspoon of mild chilli powder will give the meat lots of added flavour without making it too spicy. Be sure to toast the burger buns – they taste lovely when they're crisped up.

- Serves 4
- Ready in 20 minutes
- Suitable for freezing (burgers only)

500g pack lean minced beef
1 tsp mild chilli powder
4 burger buns

1 Put the meat in a mixing bowl, then sprinkle over the chilli powder. Season well. Mix well with your hands or use a fork. Divide the mixture into 4 equal pieces, then shape into burgers.

2 Fry the burgers on a hot griddle, or grill them on the BBQ for 5 minutes on each side. When the burgers are ready, cut the burger buns in half and warm them in the toaster, or on the BBQ.

Serve in the warm buns, with lettuce, sliced red onion, sliced tomatoes, gherkins, ketchup and mayonnaise, if you like.

Smoky chicken with warm corn and potato salad

Slicing chicken breasts in half horizontally across the middle is a good way to help them cook quickly and evenly in a dish like this.

- Serves 4
- Ready in 25 minutes
- Not suitable for freezing

500g bag new potatoes
2 large corn cobs
½ red onion, thinly sliced
juice 1 lime
2 tbsp olive oil
2 garlic cloves, crushed
½–1 tsp sweet smoked paprika
4 skinless chicken breasts, each halved across the middle to make 2 thin escalopes
small bunch coriander, roughly chopped

1 Boil the potatoes for 12 minutes, adding the corn cobs after 6 minutes, until both are tender. Drain well.

2 Meanwhile, mix the red onion with the lime juice and half the oil in a large salad bowl. Mix the remaining oil with the garlic, paprika and some seasoning in a shallow bowl. Toss in the chicken to coat.

3 Heat a griddle or frying pan, then griddle or fry the chicken for 3 minutes on each side until cooked through. Tip the potatoes into the bowl with the onions. Stand a corn cob on one end on a chopping board, then slice down the length, cutting off the kernels in strips. Mix into the potato salad with the coriander and some seasoning.

Serve with the salad and lime wedges for squeezing over, if you like.

Ham and ricotta pizza

Mozzarella is the cheese you usually find on a pizza, but here we've used ricotta instead to give a lovely creamy topping. Use either green (basil) or red (sun-dried tomato) pesto to give it an extra tang.

- Serves 4
- Ready in 25 minutes
- Not suitable for freezing

2 tbsp passata
4 ready-made pizza bases
2 slices ham, roughly torn
half a 250g tub ricotta
1 tbsp pesto
Basil leaves, to garnish (optional)

1 Spread the passata on each pizza base, then bake according to pack instructions. Just 5 minutes before the cooking time is up, scatter over the ham, dot the ricotta on top in spoonfuls and continue cooking. Season and drizzle some pesto over each pizza before serving. Garnish with basil leaves, if you like.

See photo on page 56

Lighter fish and chips

Delicious though it is, a plate of traditional fish and chips is not usually a healthy option – but if you oven-bake the chips rather than deep-frying them they're much better for you. Try this lovely batter too – the bubbles created by whisking the water and egg white will help keep it light.

▨ Serves 4
▨ Ready in 35 minutes
▨ Not suitable for freezing

800g potatoes, cut into chunky chips
3 tbsp olive oil
300g frozen peas
2 tsp lemon juice
650g skinless white fish, cut into four
50g self-raising flour, plus 1 tbsp
600ml sunflower oil, for frying
50g cornflour
125ml ice-cold sparkling water
1 egg white

1 Turn the oven to fan 200C/conventional 220C/gas 7. Cover the chips with cold water in a large pan, bring to the boil, then lower the heat and gently simmer for 4 minutes. Drain, tip onto a clean tea towel, pat dry, then leave to cool. Heat a non-stick roasting tray in the oven with 1 tbsp olive oil for 10 minutes. Transfer the chips to a bowl and toss with 1 tbsp of olive oil and some salt and pepper. Tip into the hot roasting tin in a single layer. Bake for 20 minutes, turning halfway.

2 Meanwhile, boil the peas for 4 minutes. Drain, then crush. Mix in the remaining 2 tbsp oil and the lemon juice. Season. Cover and set aside. Pat the fish dry with kitchen paper, then coat with 1 tbsp flour. Pour the sunflower oil into a heavy, non-stick wok or deep pan. Heat to 200C (a cube of bread should sizzle within 30 seconds). Mix together the flour, cornflour, a pinch of salt and pepper, then whisk in the water. Whisk the egg white until frothy and add to the batter.

3 Coat 2 pieces of fish in batter, fry in the oil for 5–6 minutes until golden, turning halfway. Lift out with a slotted spoon, drain on kitchen paper, repeat with the remaining fish. Reheat the peas and serve with the fish, chips and some lemon wedges.

easy IDEAS FOR LEFTOVERS

Don't waste them, turn them into something special

Not eaten all the food you've cooked? There's probably a really good way of 'recycling' it into another tasty recipe.

It was estimated not long ago that we throw away 8.3 million tonnes of food in the UK every year. There are lots of reasons for this and of course the possible solutions to it are complicated, but a really easy way to reduce our own individual contribution to that staggering total is to make sure we use up leftovers rather than just chucking them in the bin. Quite apart from the environmental implications of dealing with so much waste, throwing so much food away could also be making our food-shopping bills much more expensive than they need to be. If you can create tomorrow's meal using today's leftovers, it's got to be a money-saver.

So, for this chapter, we've looked at different foods that often go to waste and suggested some great ideas for using them up. If you've cooked too much veg, our *Cauliflower, broccoli and mature cheddar gratin* is just the thing, while leftover mashed potatoes make fantastic *Salmon fishcakes*. If you've got some stale bread, whizz it up in the food processor and use it as a crunchy coating for white fish fillets. Got a jar of pesto lurking in the fridge? Just 3 tablespoons are all you need to transform chicken breasts into a feast for four – the possibilities are endless!

Bulghar wheat, feta and broccoli salad, page 74

USING UP LEFTOVER VEG

It's easy to over-estimate how much veg you need to cook for Sunday lunch but if you've some left, it can easily be turned into a delicious supper to serve on Monday night. In fact, these recipes are so tasty it's worth deliberately cooking more veg than you need!

Bulghar wheat, feta and broccoli salad

■ Serves 2
■ Ready in 25 minutes
■ Not suitable for freezing

75g bulgar wheat
125g leftover cooked broccoli
1 lemon, juice only
1–2 tbsp olive oil
½ clove of crushed garlic,
100g feta
2 diced tomatoes
2 tbsp toasted pine nuts
handful of chopped flat-leaf parsley

1 Tip the bulghar wheat into a pan of salted boiling water. Take off the heat, cover and soak for 10-15 minutes. Drain well. Toss the bulghar with the broccoli, lemon juice, olive oil, crushed garlic, feta, diced tomatoes, toasted pine nuts and the chopped flat-leaf parsley. Season and serve.

See photo on page 72

Cauliflower, broccoli and mature cheddar gratin

■ Serves 2
■ Ready in 35 minutes
■ Not suitable for freezing

500g leftover cooked broccoli and
cauliflower
100g half-fat crème fraiche
50g grated mature cheddar
few tbsp snipped chives

1 Turn the oven to fan 200C/conventional 220C/gas 7. Mix the leftover veg with 100g half-fat crème fraîche, most of the cheddar and the snipped chives. Pile into 2 small ovenproof dishes and top each with a handful more cheese. Cook in the oven for 20-30 minutes, until golden and bubbling.

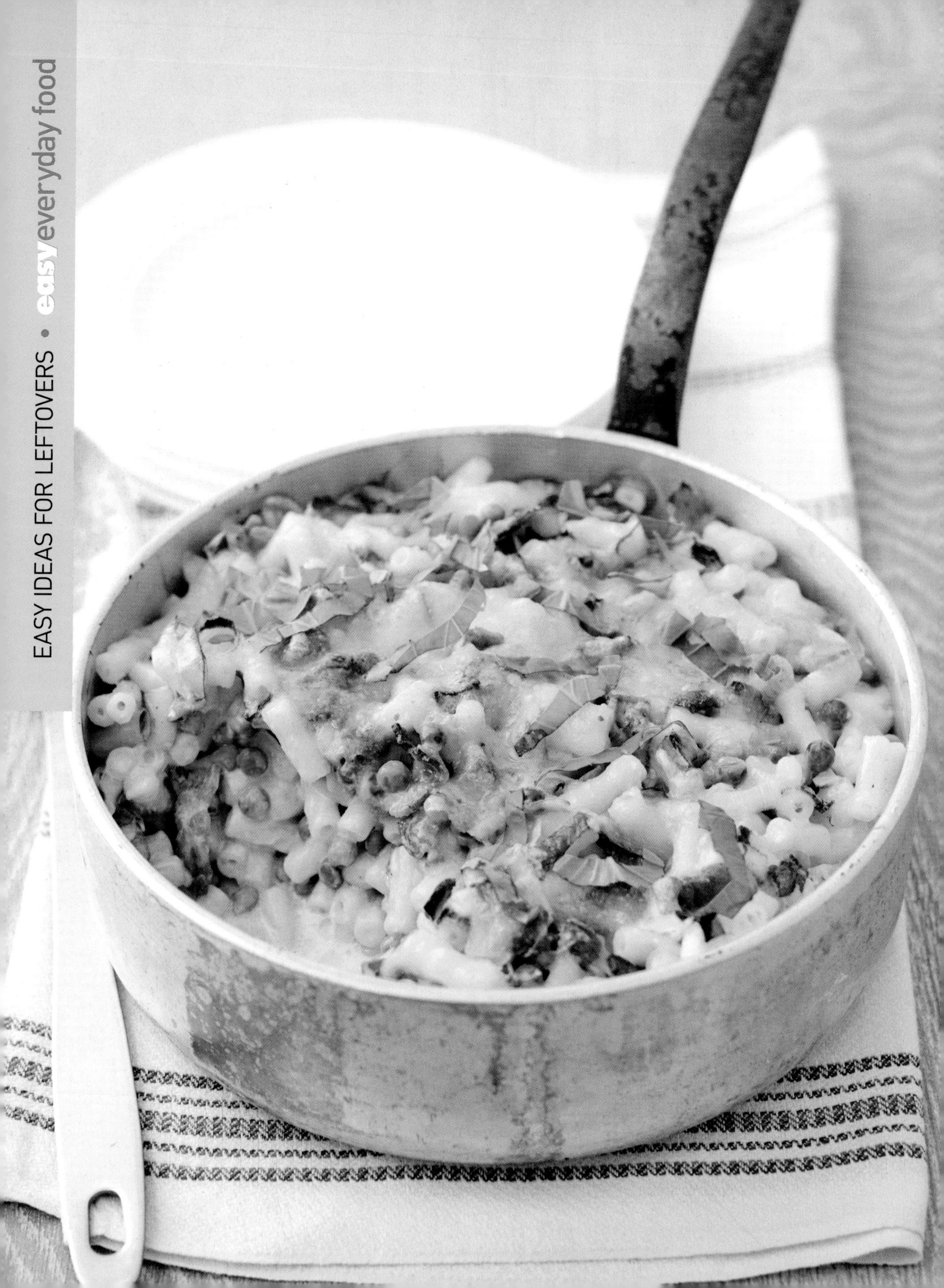

Bacon, pea and basil macaroni

Macaroni cheese is a wonderful comfort dish, but add a handful of peas and not only does it become even tastier, it's adding to your 5-a-day total as well.

▨ Serves 4
▨ Ready in 20 minutes
▨ Suitable for freezing

6 rashers streaky bacon, chopped
2 leeks, finely sliced into rings
1 tbsp vegetable oil
140g frozen peas
400g macaroni
200g pack soft cheese
85g mature cheddar, grated
1 tsp English mustard
small bunch basil, shredded

1 Fry the bacon and leeks in the oil for 10 minutes, until the bacon is golden and the leeks are soft. Tip in the peas and heat through.

2 Meanwhile, boil the pasta according to pack instructions and heat the grill to high. Reserve 150ml of the cooking water before you drain the cooked pasta, then add the reserved water, the soft cheese, half the grated cheddar and the mustard to the pan with the bacon and veg. Stir until the cheese melts into a creamy sauce. Stir in most of the basil and the pasta, then scatter with the rest of the cheddar. Grill for 2–3 minutes until the cheese melts. Scatter with the rest of the basil, to serve.

More ideas for using up leftover veg

■ Make a quick veggie curry by heating leftover veg with a sachet of Thai curry sauce and a can of coconut milk.

■ Follow the gratin recipe, on page 74, and add a savoury crumble topping made with breadcrumbs, chopped herbs and grated parmesan for a substantial meal in one.

■ Make a minty pea soup by whizzing up leftover peas in a blender with stock, a peeled and diced potato and a handful of mint then heating in a pan.

USING UP LEFTOVER BREAD

Bread that's a few days old makes better breadcrumbs than really fresh bread, so if you've got a few slices left at the end of a loaf don't waste them – whizz them up in a food processor and use them to make a crispy topping for white fish.

Crispy sesame fish

- Serves 4
- Ready in 20 minutes
- Not suitable for freezing

100g breadcrumbs, or 2 slices white bread, whizzed into crumbs
1 tbsp sesame seeds
4 skinless white fish fillets
2 tbsp natural yogurt
1 tbsp olive oil

1 Turn the oven to fan 200C/conventional 220C/gas 7. Tip the crumbs into a bowl with half the sesame seeds. Brush the fish fillets with yogurt and coat in the crumb mix. Lay on a baking tray and sprinkle over the remaining seeds. Drizzle with the olive oil, then bake for 15 minutes, until the fish is opaque and the coating is crispy.

Serve with steamed rice and green veg.

More ideas for using up bread

■ Jazz up broccoli to serve with a midweek meal by frying chopped garlic and chilli until soft, then stirring in a handful of breadcrumbs. Fry until crisp and sprinkle over the broccoli before serving.

■ For a fast supper dish, cook spaghetti according to pack instructions. Sizzle some anchovies with a chopped shallot and chilli flakes, then stir into the pasta with a spoonful of the cooking water and some chopped fresh parsley.

■ Fry breadcrumbs with pine nuts until golden, then stir in some sultanas. Season, tip in a bag of baby spinach leaves and heat until wilted. Serve with grilled meat.

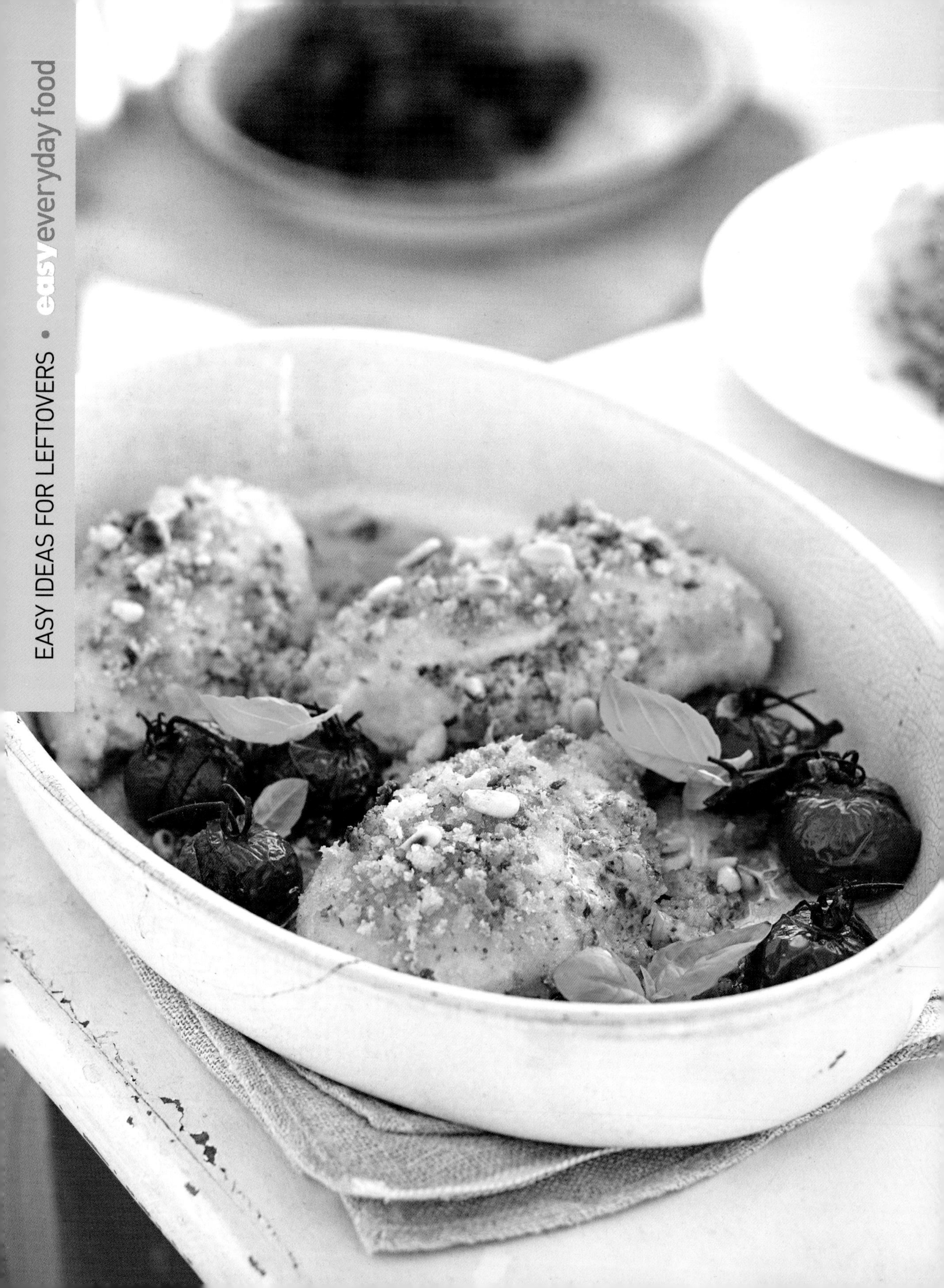

USING UP A JAR OF PESTO

When there's just a little in the bottom of a jar of ready-made pesto, it often gets pushed to the back of the fridge and forgotten about. Mix it with creamy mascarpone, though, and you've got a fantastic filling that will instantly transform plain old chicken breasts.

Creamy pesto chicken with roasted tomatoes

▨ Serves 4
▨ Ready in 40 minutes
▨ Not suitable for freezing

4 boneless, skinless chicken breasts
3 tbsp green pesto
85g mascarpone
4 tbsp olive oil
100g breadcrumbs, preferably from day-old bread
175g baby tomatoes on the vine
handful of pine nuts
handful of basil leaves

1 Turn the oven to fan 180C/conventional 200C/gas 6. Use a small, sharp knife to make a slit along the side of each chicken breast to form a pocket. Mix together the pesto and mascarpone, then carefully spoon a quarter of the mixture into each chicken breast and smooth over the opening to seal.

2 Brush a little oil over each chicken breast and season well. Tip the breadcrumbs onto a large plate and season. Put each breast on the plate and press all over with the breadcrumbs. Put in a lightly oiled, shallow baking dish along with the tomatoes (kept together on the vine in a couple of bunches). Drizzle over the remaining oil.

3 Cook in the oven for 20–25 minutes, until the chicken starts to turn golden and is cooked through. Scatter over the pine nuts and cook for 2 minutes more. Sprinkle with basil leaves.

Serve with new potatoes or crusty bread.

More ways to use up pesto

■ Transform a can or carton of tomato soup with a swirl of pesto just before serving.

■ If you're making cheese on toast, spread a little pesto onto the toast before adding the grated cheese.

■ Score a 2.5cm border around a rectangle of ready-rolled puff pastry. Spread inside the border with pesto then top with slices of goat's cheese and chopped sundried tomatoes. Bake at fan 200C/conventional 220C/gas 7 for 20 minutes until puffed up and golden.

USING UP LEFTOVER MASH

Leftover mash makes fantastic fish cakes and although you can also use leftover bread to make homemade breadcrumbs in this recipe too, for a really crispy crust they need to be very dry so ideally use pre-packed breadcrumbs from the supermarket.

Salmon fishcakes

- Serves 4
- Ready in 25 minutes
- Suitable for freezing (uncooked)

400g leftover mashed potatoes
400g flaked poached salmon
200g chopped smoked salmon (optional)
1 lemon, rind and juice
handful chopped dill or parsley
2 eggs
2 tbsp flour
100g dried breadcrumbs
vegetable oil, for frying

1 Mix the leftover mash with the poached salmon and the smoked salmon (if using), the rind and juice of the lemon and the herbs. Add some salt and pepper, then shape into 4 large or 8 small cakes. Beat the eggs in a bowl and have 1 plate ready with the flour and another with the breadcrumbs. Dust each cake in a little flour, then dip in the egg and coat in the crumbs. Fry in a little oil for 4 minutes each side until golden and crisp.

Serve with some mayonnaise, rocket and a wedge of lemon.

More ideas for using up leftover mash

- Tip a can of mixed beans in chilli sauce into an ovenproof dish then spread the leftover mash over them. Top with grated cheese and bake in a hot oven.

- For a filling lunch, heat a tub of ready-made chowder then top with spoonfuls of leftover mash warmed in the microwave.

- Turn them into a buttery colcannon. Fry chopped carrots until soft then add some shredded cabbage and continue to cook for a few more minutes. Stir into the mash with a good knob of butter and bake at fan 200C/conventional 220C/gas 7 for 20 minutes.

USING UP LEFTOVER COOKED CHICKEN

Soup is a brilliant way to make ingredients stretch that little bit further, and this is a perfect way to use up chicken leftover from a roast. If you can, shred it with a fork while it's still warm as that's easier than trying to shred cold meat.

Chicken noodle soup

■ Serves 2
■ Ready in 10 minutes
■ Not suitable for freezing

500ml low-salt vegetable stock
small piece fresh root ginger, grated
1 garlic clove, grated
2 tsp soy sauce
2 tsp sugar
85g cooked chicken, shredded
handful of mixed vegetables (try
    beansprouts, sweetcorn, carrots and
    mangetout)
150g pack straight-to-wok noodles (or you
    could use 85g dried, cooked according
    to pack instructions)
2 spring onions, sliced
juice of 1 lime

1 Put the stock, ginger, garlic, soy sauce and sugar in a pan, then simmer for 5 minutes. Add the chicken, veg and noodles, and cook for a few minutes until piping hot. Divide between 2 bowls or mugs, sprinkle with the spring onions and add the lime juice.

More ideas for using up leftover cooked chicken

■ For a speedy salad, soften noodles in boiling water, according to pack instructions. Drain and mix with cooked soya beans (from the supermarket freezer cabinet) and broccoli. Drizzle with sesame oil and soy sauce, and leave to cool. Add cooked chicken strips and serve.

■ Make mini chicken pies by lining the holes of a muffin tin with ready-made pastry and filling with cooked chicken, crème fraiche, cranberry or redcurrant sauce and seasoning. Top with pastry circles and bake at fan 200C/conventional 220C/gas 7 for 25 minutes.

USING UP LEFTOVER BACON RASHERS

If you've made a cooked breakfast at the weekend, or you've used just a couple of rashers in another recipe, you can either freeze any leftovers or put them to good use in another meal.

Leek and bacon risotto

■ Serves 4
■ Ready in 35 minutes
■ Not suitable for freezing

1.5 litres chicken stock
1 tbsp vegetable oil
4 rashers bacon, chopped
3 leeks, chopped
300g risotto rice
125ml white wine
50g parmesan, grated
snipped chives, to garnish

1 Warm the stock in a pan and leave on a low heat to keep hot. Heat the oil in a deep pan and fry the bacon for 5 minutes, until crisp. Remove and set aside. Add the leeks to the pan and cook for 5–7 minutes, then tip in the rice and stir to coat in the leeks. Pour in the wine and stir until absorbed, then add the stock, one ladle at a time, stirring and waiting until it's absorbed before adding any more liquid. Continue for about 20 minutes, until all the stock is absorbed and the rice is tender. Stir through the parmesan and return the bacon to the pan. Serve in bowls with extra parmesan and a few snipped chives on top.

More ideas for using up leftover bacon

■ Chop and fry until really crisp and use as a topping for soups.

■ Make a speedy bacon and potato sauté by frying sliced potatoes and onion, then adding chopped bacon once the potatoes are starting to soften. Continue cooking until golden and crisp.

■ For a quick snack, wrap bacon rashers around chunks of halloumi cheese and bake at fan 200C/conventional 220C/gas 7 until the bacon is crisp.

USING UP COOKED RICE

The key thing to remember with cooked rice is that if you're not using it all at once, the leftovers must be cooled quickly and then put straight in the fridge until you're ready to use it up. Keep for no more than 2 days.

Paella fried rice

- Serves 4
- Ready in 10 minutes
- Not suitable for freezing

1 tbsp vegetable oil
2 small chorizo sausages, cut into slices
1 onion, sliced
1 clove of garlic, chopped
½ tsp turmeric
600g cooked plain rice
200g frozen cooked and peeled prawns
100g frozen peas

1 Heat the oil in a frying pan. Tip in the chorizo, onion and garlic, then cook for a couple of minutes until soft. Stir in the turmeric, followed by the rice, prawns and peas and 150ml boiling water. Keep stirring until everything is warmed through and all the water has been absorbed.

Serve with lemon wedges.

More ideas for using up cooked rice

■ Make a quick salad by adding flaked canned tuna and chopped tomatoes to the cooked rice. Stir in a little mayonnaise.

■ Fry chopped onions and garlic until soft then add a teaspoon of ground cumin and some bashed cardamom pods. Fry for a minute more. Add some shredded turkey and the cooked rice then heat until piping hot in the microwave.

■ Make a veggie rice stir-fry by frying a chopped onion and garlic until soft. Add some curry powder and tomato ketchup, then stir in the cooked rice and a glass of water, and cook for 5 minutes until piping hot.

PART TWO

easy weekend food

When you've got a little more time to spend in the kitchen, these recipes are perfect

In our Weekend section we've allowed ourselves the luxury of recipes that, although still really easy to make, might take a little longer in the oven.

You'll find roasts here that take just a few minutes to prepare and then they can sit in the oven cooking while you get on with other things. An hour or two later, just add the veg and you've got a meal to be proud of.

There's more time for baking at the weekend too, and we've got lots of ideas, both sweet and savoury (and don't miss the birthday cake, hot cross buns and cupcakes in Easy Occasions).

When the weather's good, a barbecue or picnic is the order of the day and there is something here for all occasions – whether you've planned well in advance or just decided at the last minute to light the coals or get the picnic basket out of the cupboard.

And, of course, the weekend is the time to invite friends and family, and our mix-and-match ideas will see you sailing through the cooking with ease!

Mango and passion fruit roulade, page 185

easy
BRUNCHES
The perfect start to a lazy weekend

After a long lie-in, what could be better than a mid-morning breakfast or early lunch?

There's something very decadent about brunch. More substantial than a normal breakfast but served earlier than lunch, it takes you nicely into the weekend. It's ideal for casual entertaining, giving you a chance to show off your cooking skills without swallowing up much of the day.

Our selection of recipes in this chapter ranges from light bites like *Quick croque monsieur* if you fancy something savoury, to *Ricotta pancakes with oranges and honey* if you prefer something sweet. If you're ravenous, *Chorizo hash with poached egg* or *Ham and eggy bread with salsa* would be a good choice, all washed down with a delicious *Super smoothie* and finished off with a *Medley of summer fruits* (with or without a dash of alcohol in the syrup, depending on what sort of occasion it is!).

Baked eggs with ham, tomatoes and cheese, page 98

Quick croque monsieur

This is a classic snack that you can buy in cafes and bakeries all over France and it makes a great breakfast or brunch. Add a fried or poached egg on top and you have an even more substantial croque madame.

- Serves 2
- Ready in 10 minutes
- Not suitable for freezing

2 slices wholemeal bread
1 egg, beaten
large handful of grated cheddar
2 slices ham, cut into strips
pinch English mustard powder

1 Heat the grill to high and toast the bread lightly on both sides. While the bread is toasting, combine all the other ingredients in a bowl. Press the cheesy mix onto the toast, then put under the grill for 3–4 minutes, until golden and bubbling. Cut into halves and serve.

Chorizo hash with poached egg

A hash is traditionally made with corned beef, but using spicy chorizo gives it a modern twist.

- Serves 2 (easily multiplied)
- Ready in 25 minutes
- Not suitable for freezing

300g new potatoes, quartered
2 tbsp olive oil
40g chorizo, cut into strips
1 red chilli, deseeded and finely chopped
½ small bunch parsley, chopped
2 eggs, poached

1 Boil the potatoes until tender, drain and cool. Heat the oil in a large, non-stick frying pan and fry, turning frequently, until golden and crisp. Add the chorizo and chilli, and fry for 3–4 minutes more, until the chorizo is crisp. Season, then stir through the parsley. Serve the potatoes topped with the poached eggs.

Try these ideas too

■ Instead of ham, use chopped grilled bacon.

■ Add a dash of Worcestershire sauce instead of the mustard powder.

■ Instead of cheddar, use red leicester cheese and top with hot baked beans just before serving.

■ Top with thin slices of mozzarella before grilling.

Ricotta pancakes with oranges

Serve the pancakes in a pile, topped with the orange slices, a drizzle of honey and a sprinkling of nuts. If you like, you can add a handful of juicy sultanas to the batter in step 1.

■ Serves 4
■ Ready in 15 minutes
■ Not suitable for freezing

200g plain flour
1 tsp baking powder
1 egg, beaten
200ml semi-skimmed milk
220g tub ricotta
1 tbsp sunflower oil
handful of pistachio nuts, roughly chopped
2 oranges, peeled and sliced into rounds
clear honey, to drizzle

1 Put the flour, baking powder and a pinch of salt into a large bowl. Make a well in the middle, then pour in the egg and a splash of milk. Using a wooden spoon, gradually draw the flour into the liquid until you have a lump-free batter. Mix in the rest of the milk, then beat in the ricotta.

2 Heat a large, non-stick frying pan and add the oil. Swirl it around the pan, then tip out any excess into a heatproof bowl. Spoon in 3–4 tbsps of the batter, spaced well apart, to make pancakes about 10cm across. Cook on a medium heat for 2 minutes until bubbles appear on the surface. Flip over with a palette knife and cook for 2 more minutes, until golden. Set aside and keep warm while you cook the rest.

Ham and eggy bread with salsa

This is great served with spoonfuls of ready-made tomato salsa, or make your own (see recipe below). In France, this recipe is known as 'pain perdu'.

■ Serves 1 (easily multiplied)
■ Ready in 10 minutes
■ Not suitable for freezing

1 tsp butter, plus extra for frying
2 thick slices bread
2 slices ham
1 egg
2 tbsp milk
1 tsp olive oil

1 Lightly butter and sandwich the slices of bread with the ham. Cut the sandwich in half diagonally. In a shallow bowl, beat the egg and milk together, then season. Melt a small knob of butter and the olive oil in a non-stick frying pan, until the butter foams.

2 Dip the sandwich halves into the egg mix on both sides, then add to the pan. Cook over a medium heat for 2 minutes on each side or until set and golden.

Make your own tomato salsa

■ Grill 4 halved tomatoes, cut-side up, for 3–4 minutes, until the skins start to blacken. Transfer to a bowl, mash with a fork and stir in 1 finely chopped red chilli, 1 finely chopped clove of garlic, 2 tbsp chopped basil, a pinch of brown sugar, 2 tbsp olive oil and 1 tbsp red wine vinegar.

Tomato and mushroom stacks

Treat the family to this veggie brunch, perfect for a relaxed Sunday morning. If you can't find ready-made polenta (which comes in a ready-to-use slab and is not to be confused with the powdered type), you can use toasted English muffins instead.

- Serves 4
- Ready in 40 minutes
- Not suitable for freezing

500g pack ready-made polenta
½ tsp dried oregano
25g grated parmesan
50g cheddar, grated
4 tbsp olive oil
4 large flat mushrooms, stalks removed
400g ripe tomatoes, roughly chopped
1 clove of garlic, finely chopped

1 Turn the oven to fan 200C/conventional 220C/gas 7. Cut the polenta into twelve 1cm thick slices and stack in 4 overlapping piles in a roasting tin. Sprinkle with oregano and most of the cheeses. Pour the oil into a bowl, season and brush a little over each mushroom. Put one mushroom, stalk-side up, on each polenta stack.

2 Tip the tomatoes and garlic into the remaining oil. Spoon the tomatoes and their juices in and around the mushrooms and polenta, then season some more. Sprinkle over the remaining cheese and roast for 30 minutes, until the mushrooms are tender. Serve hot.

Baked eggs with ham, tomatoes and cheese

Instead of grabbing a slice of toast in the morning, get the whole family to sit down together for breakfast at the weekend every now and again – if this doesn't tempt them, nothing will! If you don't have individual dishes to cook this in, use 1 large baking dish and bake for 20 minutes.

- Serves 4
- Ready in 15 minutes
- Not suitable for freezing

knob of butter, plus extra for buttering
227g can chopped tomatoes
4 thick slices ham
4 eggs
50g grated cheddar
2 slices bread

1 Turn the oven to fan 160C/ conventional 180C/gas 4. Lightly butter 4 individual oval ramekins (or ovenproof dishes). Spoon 2 tbsps of the tomatoes into the bottom of each dish, followed by a slice of ham. Crack an egg over each, season and finish with a sprinkling of cheese. Bake for 10 minutes or until the eggs are cooked to your liking.

2 Meanwhile, toast the bread and lightly butter, then cut each slice into 4 triangles. Tuck 2 triangles into each dish before serving.

See photo on page 92

Super smoothie

Packed with goodness, filling and delicious too – a great way to start the day.

▓ Serves 2 (easily multiplied)
▓ Ready in 5 minutes
▓ Not suitable for freezing

150g punnet blueberries (defrosted if frozen)
2 bananas
50g medium porridge oats
½ 500g pot natural yogurt
300ml semi-skimmed milk
2 tbsp clear honey
1 tsp poppy seeds
grating of nutmeg, to decorate

1 Tip the blueberries into a blender and whizz into a purée. Pour the contents into a bowl, set aside, then rinse the blender.

2 Chop the bananas into chunks, then add to the blender with the rest of the ingredients, except the nutmeg, and blend until smooth. Pour some of the banana mixture into 2 large glasses, top with a spoonful of blueberry purée, then more of the banana. Continue until you have used up both mixtures, finishing with a swirl of purée. Grate the nutmeg over to serve.

Medley of summer fruits

We've used dessert wine and Champagne here, which makes it ideal for a really special occasion, but you could use diluted elderflower cordial instead, if you prefer.

▓ Serves 4
▓ Ready in 25 minutes, plus 4 hours chilling
▓ Suitable for freezing

250ml Sauternes or dessert wine
250ml cabernet sauvignon or dry red wine
50g caster sugar
1 vanilla pod, split, seeds scraped out
12 mint leaves, roughly chopped, plus sprigs to serve
6 basil leaves, roughly chopped
250g mixed summer fruits (such as fresh raspberries, blackberries and sliced peaches)
½ Charentais melon, scooped into 12 balls
200g fresh strawberries, halved and quartered
100ml chilled pink Champagne (optional)

1 In a large pan, bring the 2 wines, sugar and vanilla pod to the boil. Put the mint and basil in the centre of a small piece of muslin and tie with string to make a bag, then add to the pan with a few grinds of freshly ground black pepper.

2 Remove from heat and leave to cool to room temperature. Remove the muslin bag, add the summer fruits, melon and any other fruit you're using, apart from the strawberries, then chill for 4 hours.

3 About 2 hours before serving, add the strawberries to the syrup. Serve in a large serving bowl or 4 individual bowls. Pour about 2 tbsp of the pink Champagne over just before serving, if using.

easy
SUNDAY LUNCHES

Perfect recipes to enjoy with family and friends

The traditional Sunday roast seems to have gone out of fashion recently, but we want to bring it back!

The wonderful smell of a joint roasting in the oven on Sunday morning sums up what weekends are all about. So don't just save roasts for special occasions, make every Sunday a special day.

Chicken is probably most people's favourite roast and our 'Ultimate' recipe is a real can't-go-wrong method that we're sure you'll use again and again once you've tried it. Prefer beef? A rib of beef will look after itself once it's in the oven, so nothing could be simpler. Or how about pork with perfect crackling?

You'll need a good gravy to go with the meat of course. Our pork recipe includes a lovely honey mustard gravy, or try our *Rich gravy* with any other meats.

Just two words of advice here, though: firstly, even the best cook in the world can't make a good roast out of poor-quality meat, so do try to buy the best you can afford – you'll really notice the difference in the taste. And, secondly, whatever kind of meat you're roasting, don't be tempted to skip the resting stage. It'll make the meat easier to carve and the flavour and texture will be much better.

Ultimate roast chicken, page 104

Roast rib of beef

Nothing beats roast beef for Sunday lunch and, so long as you choose good-quality meat, all you need to do is flavour the meat with some herbs and seasoning. Always check red meat just before the cooking time is up – it's much better to find it's too rare and then put it back in the oven for 5 minutes than to over-cook it.

- Serves 8
- Ready in 1 hour 45 minutes, plus 20 minutes resting time
- Not suitable for freezing

2.5kg piece boneless rib of beef
2 tbsp mixed peppercorns
2 tbsp fresh thyme leaves
1 tsp coarse sea salt
1 tsp olive oil

1 Turn the oven to fan 210C/conventional 230C/gas 8. Wipe the meat with damp kitchen paper. Crush the peppercorns, thyme leaves and sea salt using a mortar and pestle. Brush the oil over the beef and press on the peppercorn and thyme mixture.

2 Roast uncovered for 20 minutes, then lower the heat to fan 170C/conventional 190C/gas 5. Roast for a further 1 hour 15 minutes for rare (30 minutes per kg). For medium to well-done, roast for 15–25 minutes more. When the meat is done, take it out of the roasting tin and leave it to rest for 20 minutes. Save the juices from the pan to make the gravy.

Perfect Yorkshire puddings

Make the batter while the meat is roasting, then cook the pud while it's resting.

- Makes 8 large puddings
- Ready in 45 minutes
- Suitable for freezing

8 tbsp sunflower oil
2 eggs
1 egg white
115g plain flour mixed with ¼ tsp salt
50ml water
175ml full-fat milk

1 Turn the oven to fan 200C/conventional 220C/gas 7. Spoon a scant tablespoon of oil into each hole of two 4-hole Yorkshire pudding trays. Put in the oven for 15 minutes.

2 Whisk the whole eggs and the egg white in a large bowl. Start to add the flour, a couple of spoonfuls at a time, beating well with the whisk as you go, to keep the lumps at bay and the mixture smooth. The mixture will thicken to a sloppy paste. Mix the water and milk together, then gradually pour in the liquid, again a little at a time, whisking as you go, until it is smooth and a little thinner than double cream. Pour the batter into a jug.

3 Carefully lift the tin of hot fat out of the oven, using oven gloves, and quickly pour a little batter into each tin so each is three-quarters full. The batter should start to sizzle in the hot fat as it is poured in. Bake for 15–20 minutes, until the Yorkshires are tall, golden, puffed and crisp on the sides. Pour off any excess fat and serve. Once cooled, they can be frozen. Reheat from frozen at fan 160C/conventional 180C/gas 4 for 4–5 minutes.

Ultimate roast chicken

A 1.5kg chicken should be perfectly roasted after 1 hour 20 minutes at fan 170C/conventional 190C/gas 5, but oven temperatures do vary, so always test the chicken as per step 2. Take the chicken out of the fridge 1 hour before cooking to bring it up to room temperature. (This applies to any meat you are roasting.)

- Serves 4
- Ready in 1 hour 35 minutes, plus 20 minutes resting time
- Not suitable for freezing

1 onion, roughly chopped
2 carrots, roughly chopped
1.5kg whole chicken
1 lemon, halved
small bunch of thyme (optional)
25g soft butter

1 Turn the oven to fan 170C/conventional 190C/gas 5. Have a shelf ready in the middle of the oven without any shelves above it. Scatter the vegetables over the base of a roasting tin. Season the cavity of the chicken liberally with salt and pepper, then stuff with the lemon halves and thyme, if using. Sit the chicken on the vegetables, smother the breast and legs all over with the butter, then season the outside with salt and pepper.

2 Put in the oven and leave, undisturbed, for 1 hour 20 minutes. To check the chicken is cooked, pierce the thickest part of the thigh with a skewer – the juices should run clear. If they are still pink, cook for 5 minutes and test again. Remove the tin from the oven and, using a pair of tongs, lift the chicken on to a dish or board to rest for 15–20 minutes before carving. As you lift the chicken, let any juices pour out into the roasting tin and save them to make the gravy. **See photo on page 100**

Rich gravy

This gravy is great to serve with any roast meat, although if you're cooking lamb you might want to replace the redcurrant jelly with mint jelly (not mint sauce though, as that's too vinegary). You could also swap 225ml of the stock for red wine if you have some open.

- Serves 10 (easily halved)
- Ready in 10 minutes
- Not suitable for freezing

5 tbsp pan juices from the roast
2 tbsp plain flour
825ml hot stock
2 tbsp redcurrant or bramble jelly

1 Heat the pan juices on the hob. Sprinkle in the flour and cook, stirring, until rich brown in colour. Gradually pour in the stock. Bring to the boil, stirring until slightly thickened. Simmer for 5 minutes, continuing to stir. Stir in the redcurrant or bramble jelly and allow to melt.

Broccoli with garlic and chilli breadcrumbs

This spicy breadcrumb topping is also delicious sprinkled over cauliflower or leeks and it's worth making extra if you've got lots of bread to use up – freeze what you don't need in food bags and use them straight from frozen.

- Serves 4
- Ready in 20 minutes
- Not suitable for freezing

500g broccoli
2 tbsp olive oil
knob of butter
2 small cloves of garlic, finely chopped
1 small red chilli, deseeded and finely chopped
50g white breadcrumbs

1 Steam the broccoli for 5 minutes until tender. Meanwhile, heat the oil and butter in a pan, then fry the garlic and chilli for 1 minute. Add the breadcrumbs, then fry for 5 minutes until crisp. Season the broccoli, arrange in a dish, then scatter over the spicy breadcrumbs and serve.

St Clement's carrots

Baby and new season carrots are lovely boiled or steamed just as they are, but older carrots can often do with a bit of a boost to bring out their flavour and this recipe does that really well. If clementines aren't available, you can use an orange instead.

- Serves 6
- Ready in 50 minutes
- Not suitable for freezing

800g carrots, peeled and trimmed
3 clementines, grated rind plus a few slices
1 tbsp olive oil
1 tbsp butter
2 lemons, grated rind

1 Turn the oven to fan 180C/conventional 200C/gas 6 and bring a large pan of water to the boil. Cut the carrots lengthways into halves or quarters, depending on their size. Tip the carrots into the pan, wait for the water to simmer again, then cook for 4 minutes.

2 Drain well, then tip into a large roasting tin. While the carrots are still hot, gently toss with the clementine rind, olive oil, butter, some seasoning, the grated lemon rind and a few clementine slices. Poke the slices in among the carrots, so they're not left on the edges of the tin. Roast for 40 minutes, until the carrots are golden and tender.

Crunchy roast potatoes

Who doesn't love roast potatoes with their Sunday lunch? The secret to getting them really crisp is to make sure the fat is very hot before you add the potatoes to the tin – put them in carefully because if the oil's hot enough, it will sizzle vigorously. Goose fat will give really rich roasties, but oil will crisp them just as well.

- Serves 8
- Ready in 1 hour
- Not suitable for freezing

2.5kg even-sized potatoes, peeled and halved if large
5 tbsp sunflower oil or goose fat
salt, to sprinkle

1 Turn the oven to fan 180C/conventional 200C/gas 6. Boil the potatoes for 10 minutes, then drain. Rough up their surfaces with a fork, or by shaking them in the pan with the lid on.

2 Meanwhile, spoon the oil or goose fat into a large roasting tin and leave to heat on the top shelf of the oven. Tip in the potatoes carefully and turn them until they are evenly coated in the fat. Put on the top shelf of the oven and roast for 50 minutes, turning every now and then, until crisp and golden. Sprinkle with salt to serve.

Crisp roast pork with honey mustard gravy

The perfect time to make gravy to go with your roast is while the meat is resting – and it means you can use all the delicious meat juices from the roasting tin too. Here we're made a lovely sweet but tangy gravy that's ready in just a few minutes.

- Serves 4
- Ready in 2 hours 40 minutes
- Not suitable for freezing

2kg pork loin, bone in, fat scored
1 tbsp olive oil
100ml hot chicken stock
1 tbsp wholegrain mustard
1 tbsp clear honey
1 tsp finely chopped thyme leaves

1 Turn the oven to fan 220C/conventional 240C/gas 9. Pat the pork all over with kitchen paper. Lightly rub all over with the olive oil and sprinkle liberally with salt. Cook for 20 minutes, turn the oven down to fan 170C/conventional 190C/gas 5, then cook for 30 minutes per 500g (about 2 hours). Remove from the tin, put on a serving plate and loosely cover with foil.

2 Pour off any excess fat from the tin. Add the stock to the tin, then stir to incorporate the meat juices and sticky bits at the bottom. Pour through a sieve into a small pan. Add the mustard, honey and thyme, plus the juices from the resting meat. Stir and simmer for 5 minutes until it is starting to turn syrupy. Serve alongside the pork.

Rack of lamb with an apricot and mustard crust

This is a great recipe once the new season's lamb comes into the supermarkets in spring. Bring it to the table to carve because it looks so effective, and it's really easy to portion out – just cut between the bones. You can prepare the lamb up to the end of step 2, then chill for up to 3 hours before roasting.

▓ Serves 6 with leftovers
▓ Ready in 2 hours
▓ Not suitable for freezing

140g fresh white breadcrumbs
4 tbsp chopped fresh parsley
1 tbsp chopped fresh rosemary
1 tsp grated lemon rind
8 ready-to-eat dried apricots, roughly chopped
2 tbsp olive oil
1 medium egg, beaten
1 tbsp dijon mustard, plus 2 tsp extra
2 racks of lamb, each with 6 chops, total weight about 1.2kg
2 cloves of garlic, chopped
300ml red wine
300ml hot lamb stock
1–2 tbsp apricot jam
knob of butter, chilled

1 Turn the oven to fan 200C/conventional 220C/gas 7. Mix together the breadcrumbs, parsley, rosemary, lemon rind, apricots, oil and egg. Spread ½ tbsp of mustard over the inside curves of the lamb, sprinkle with the garlic and season. Spoon ½ of the crumb mixture on top of 1 rack. Press the other rack on top, enclosing the filling and crossing the bones. Tie string around the meat vertically to hold the racks together. Spread ½ tbsp mustard on the outside of the racks and press on the remaining crumb mixture. Put the tied racks in a roasting tin.

2 Roast the lamb for 10 minutes, then lower the heat to fan 170C/conventional 190C/gas 5 and cook for 1–1¼ hours, depending on how well done you like it. (If the bone ends begin to burn, cover them with foil.) Transfer the lamb to a serving plate, cover loosely with foil and put the roasting tin on the hob.

3 Add the wine to the tin and bubble rapidly for 3–4 minutes, until it has reduced to a syrup. Add the hot lamb stock, then stir in the extra 2 tsp of the mustard and the jam to taste. Cook for a few minutes until the jam melts. Whisk in the butter and season to taste. Remove the string, then slice the lamb into cutlets. Serve with the red wine sauce.

Melty mushroom Wellington

The key thing with this recipe is to make sure you get rid of as much water as possible from the spinach in step 2. Drain it in the colander and then press down on it with the back of a spoon to squeeze out any excess – this will ensure the filling is lovely and moist rather than soggy.

■ Serves 4
■ Ready in 1 hour 10 minutes
■ Suitable for freezing (assembled, but not baked)

4 large field mushrooms
4 tbsp olive oil
1 clove of garlic, chopped
about 400g spinach leaves
a dusting of flour
1 tbsp thyme leaves
500g block all-butter puff pastry
140g Stilton, sliced
1 egg, beaten

1 Turn the oven to 200C fan/conventional 220C/ gas 7. Remove the stalks from the mushrooms and discard. Heat half the oil in a large frying pan and sizzle the mushrooms for 3–4 minutes on each side, until golden and cooked through – add a drop more oil if needed. Lift the mushrooms out onto kitchen paper to drain.

2 Put the same pan back on the heat with the rest of the oil. Fry the garlic for a moment, add the spinach to the pan, then cook for 2–3 minutes over a high heat, until completely wilted. Season with salt and pepper, then tip the spinach into a large sieve to drain thoroughly.

3 On a lightly floured surface, scattered with the thyme leaves, roll the pastry out to the thickness of a £1 coin. Using a saucer and a larger-sized plate, cut out 4 circles about 5cm wider than the mushrooms (for the bottoms) and 4 circles about 10cm wider (for the tops), re-rolling the trimmings if you need to.

4 Put the 4 smaller circles on a baking tray and top each with a quarter of the spinach, making sure the pile of spinach isn't wider than the mushrooms. Top the spinach with a slice of cheese, then a mushroom, smooth-side up, and top the mushroom with another slice of cheese. Brush the border of each circle with egg, then gently stretch the larger circle over the mushroom, trying not to trap any air. Press the edges together with a fork, trim them with a knife if you like, then brush each generously with beaten egg. Bake for 40 minutes until golden, then leave to cool for a few minutes before serving.

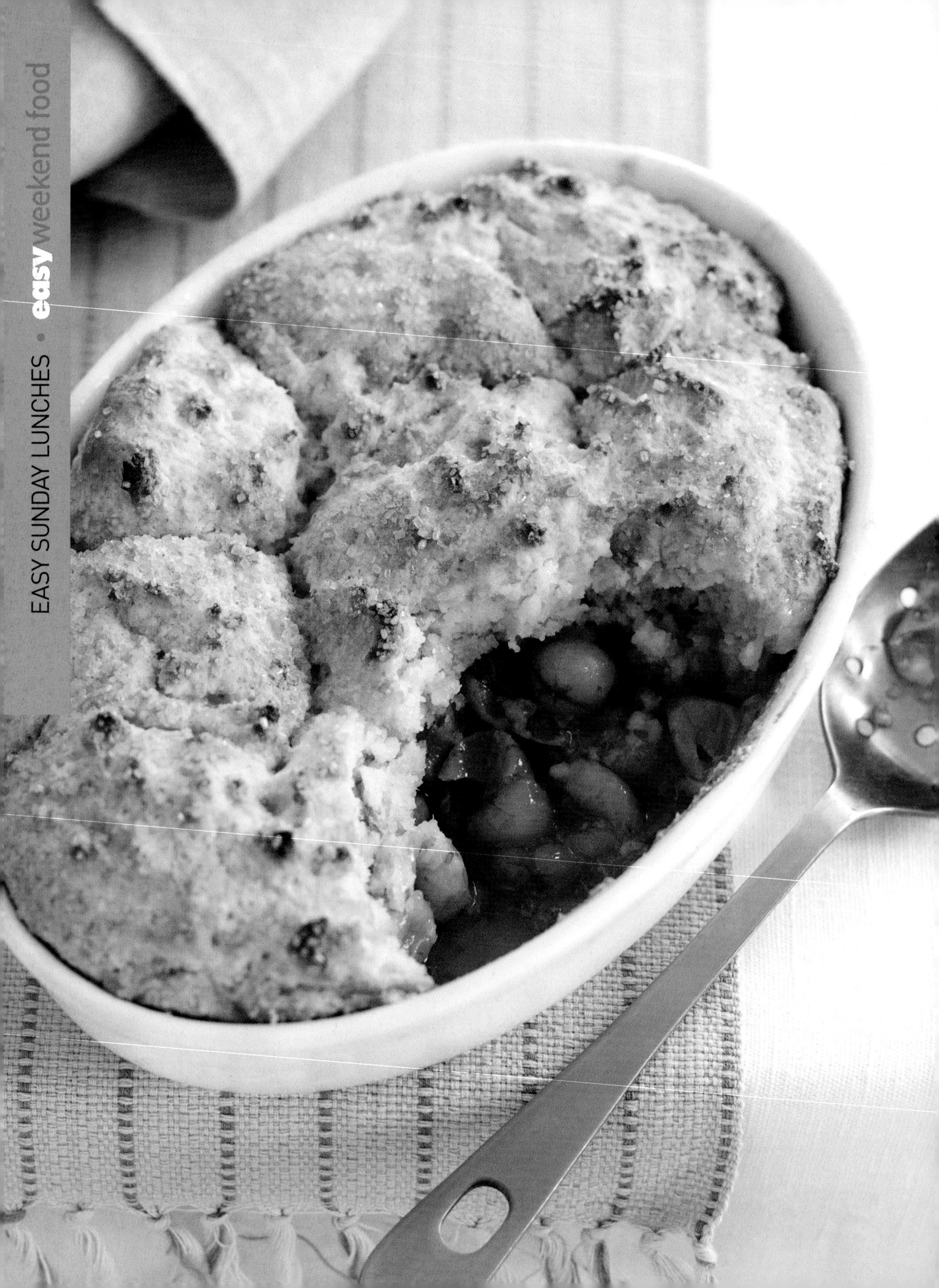

Easy gooseberry cobbler

Gooseberries are a real treat because they're only in season for a short while in mid-summer, but you can make this cobbler with plums too (reduce the amount of sugar to taste in step 1 though, as plums are less tart than gooseberries). If you can't find buttermilk, use low-fat natural yogurt, thinned down slightly with a little cold water.

- Serves 6
- Ready in 40 minutes
- Suitable for freezing (after baking)

750g gooseberries, washed, topped and tailed
125g caster sugar
1 tsp grated root ginger
3 tbsp elderflower cordial
140g plain flour
2 tsp baking powder
25g butter
150ml buttermilk
1 tbsp demerara sugar

1 Turn the oven to fan 170C/conventional 190C/gas 5. Put the gooseberries, 100g caster sugar, ginger and elderflower cordial in a pan with 4 tbsp water and cook, covered, for 5 minutes until the berries begin to pop. Tip into a baking dish.

2 Sift the flour, baking powder and a pinch of salt into a mixing bowl. Rub in the butter until the mixture looks like breadcrumbs, then stir in the remaining caster sugar. Mix in the buttermilk to give a soft, sticky dough. Spoon on top of the gooseberries, then sprinkle with the demerara sugar. Bake for 25 minutes, or until golden brown and crusty. Stand for 5 minutes before serving.

Serve with ice cream, fromage frais or custard.

Frozen lemon and ginger yogurt terrine

Get this out of the freezer when you serve the main course as it will be a lot easier to slice if it's been at room temperature for 20 minutes or so. You can make the terrine up to 2 weeks ahead and keep it in the freezer.

- Serves 6
- Takes 30 minutes, plus freezing
- Suitable for freezing

500g tub Greek yogurt
300ml tub double cream, lightly whipped
grated rind of 1 lemon
4 pieces stem ginger in syrup from a jar, shredded, and 2 tbsp of the syrup (plus a little extra ginger and syrup to serve)
3 tbsp ginger wine (optional)
10 ginger biscuits, crushed

1 Line a small loaf tin with cling film. Mix together the yogurt, cream, lemon rind, ginger pieces, ginger syrup and ginger wine (if using). Put a third of the yogurt mixture into the bottom of the tin, then add half the biscuits. Add another third of yogurt, then top with the rest of the biscuits. Finish with the remaining yogurt mixture. Freeze for at least 4 hours or overnight.

2 Turn out and leave for 20–30 minutes before cutting into slices to serve. Serve with a little extra ginger syrup poured over and a few extra pieces of ginger.

Easiest-ever bread pudding

The perfect dessert for a cold winter's afternoon, this is delicious served with a shop-bought berry compote and a spoonful of crème fraiche. Don't be tempted to use skimmed milk here – you need the rich taste of whole milk.

- Serves 4
- Takes 10 minutes, plus 35 minutes in the oven
- Not suitable for freezing

600ml tub fresh custard
150ml whole milk
140g white bread
50g raisins or dried cherries
butter, for greasing
5–7 tbsp caster sugar

1 Turn the oven to fan 120C/conventional 140C/gas 1. Stir the custard and milk together. Trim the crusts from the bread, cut into triangles, then put in a large bowl with the raisins or dried cherries. Pour over the custard mixture, then carefully stir everything together so all the pieces of bread are coated. Lightly grease a small ovenproof dish with butter, then spoon in the mixture.

2 Cook for 30–35 minutes, until there is just a slight wobble in the centre of the custard. Sprinkle over the sugar to cover the surface, then put under a hot grill for 1–2 minutes, until the sugar starts to melt and caramelise.

easy ENTERTAINING

Invite friends round for a casual supper and show off your cooking skills

Making a meal for friends needn't be daunting with our easy mix-and-match starters, mains and puds.

When we talk to *Easy Cook* readers about inviting people to supper, there are two things they often say: either that they never do it because they're not confident enough in their cooking abilities, or that they've done it a few times but it was such hard work and so stressful that they're not keen to repeat the experience.

Our advice is always that, if you keep things simple, entertaining can be just as much fun for the cook as it is for the guests. Plan your meal in advance, have a practice run so you're confident that you know exactly what to do on the day, and prep as much as you can ahead of

time so you've only got finishing touches to do once your guests arrive.

We've got recipes here for every occasion, from a simple tomato soup that has a gremolata garnish (it looks fancy but is very easy to make) to a refreshing *Chicken and orange salad* that's great to serve at summer dinner parties. Follow these with everything from a fish curry to exotically flavoured *Five-spice beef with black bean sauce*, and if you've got vegetarian guests our *Pea, tarragon and cream cheese pithiviers* looks great and will go down well with everyone.

Pan-fried pork with crème fraiche and prunes, page 126

Tomato soup with gremolata

Gremolata is a tasty garnish made of lemon, olive oil, garlic and parsley – it adds lots of extra flavour to soups like this (and it's good with grilled white fish too). For an ultra-smooth soup, you can pass the liquid through a fine sieve after you've whizzed it in the blender.

- Serves 4
- Ready in 50 minutes
- Not suitable for freezing

1 onion, chopped
4 cloves of garlic, crushed
7 tbsp olive oil
2kg tomatoes
2 tbsp sugar
2 tbsp white wine vinegar
grated rind and juice of 1 lemon
a bunch of flat-leaf parsley, finely chopped

1 In a large shallow pan, fry the onion and garlic in 4 tbsp of olive oil on a low heat for 8 minutes, but do not brown. Roughly chop the tomatoes and add along with the sugar, vinegar, 750ml water and seasoning. Bring to the boil and simmer for 35 minutes, stirring from time to time.

2 Whizz the soup with a hand or stick blender until smooth.

3 Mix together the lemon rind and juice, the remaining 3 tbsp of olive oil, garlic and parsley, then serve swirled into the soup.

Chicken and orange salad

A lovely, refreshing starter that's ideal for a summer dinner party or lunch. Don't make it too far in advance, or the avocado and fennel may start to brown.

- Serves 2
- Ready in 10 minutes
- Not suitable for freezing

150g pack green beans, trimmed
1 fennel bulb
1 large avocado
100g bag watercress, roughly chopped
2 oranges
2 tbsp olive oil
2 cooked skinless chicken breasts, shredded

1 Cook the beans in a large pan of boiling salted water for 4–5 minutes. Cool under cold water and put in a bowl. Finely slice the fennel bulb, cutting away the core, and add to the bowl. Peel and slice the avocado and add this to the bowl, along with the watercress. Peel the oranges, cut out the segments, and add to the salad, catching the juices for the dressing.

2 Squeeze the rest of the orange juice into a small bowl with the reserved juice and mix with the olive oil to make a dressing. Toss the salad in the dressing and scatter over the chicken.

Scallops with fresh tomato sauce

To save a lot of last-minute rushing about, you can make the sauce up to 2 hours in advance, then put it on serving plates, cover with cling film and leave at room temperature until you're ready to cook the scallops.

▧ Serves 6
▧ Ready in 35 minutes
▧ Not suitable for freezing

150ml olive oil, plus a drizzle extra
2 cloves of garlic, very finely sliced
2 tsp coriander seeds
550g ripe tomatoes
4 tbsp red wine vinegar
small handful each of basil, coriander and
**   parsley leaves, finely chopped**
18 large scallops

1 Warm the oil, garlic and coriander seeds very gently in a pan, then set aside. Make a small cross in the bottom of each tomato and tip into a large bowl. Pour a kettleful of boiling water over the tomatoes and leave for about 10 seconds, then drain and cool under cold water. Peel and halve the tomatoes and squeeze out the seeds, then roughly chop the flesh. Tip the tomatoes into a bowl and season with salt and pepper. Stir in the vinegar, flavoured oil and the herbs, then set aside for at least 20 minutes so all the flavours mingle.

2 Heat a pan until very hot, toss the scallops with a drizzle of olive oil and sear for about 1 minute on each side, until nicely caramelised. Spoon a pool of tomatoes onto plates and top each with 3 scallops.

Fish curry

Invite friends round and turn Saturday night into curry night with this quick-to-prepare recipe that's packed with flavour.

▧ Serves 4
▧ Ready in 25 minutes
▧ Not suitable for freezing

1 onion, finely sliced
1 tsp olive oil
2 tbsp madras curry paste
two 400g cans chopped tomatoes
450g white fish fillets cut into large chunks
small handful of coriander leaves

1 Fry the onion in the oil in a large pan until soft, then add the curry paste and cook for 2 minutes. Stir in the tomatoes, then simmer for 10 minutes until reduced and thickened. Add the fish and gently simmer for 3–4 minutes, until the fish is cooked through. Scatter with the coriander.

Serve with naan bread or steamed basmati rice.

Prawn and tomato spaghetti

This works well as a hearty lunch or a light supper and is perfect for casual entertaining. Better still, as it's all made in one-pot there's not much washing-up afterwards. Fontina is a semi-hard Italian cheese that melts really well. If you can't find it, use cheddar instead.

- Serves 4
- Ready in 40 minutes
- Not suitable for freezing

2 tbsp olive oil
handful of fresh basil leaves, torn
2 cloves of garlic, crushed
1kg plum tomatoes, chopped
2 tbsp tomato purée
400g wholewheat spaghetti
500g raw peeled king prawns (thawed if frozen)
50g fontina cheese
50g parmesan
basil leaves, to garnish (optional)

1 Heat the oil in a deep-sided frying pan, then gently fry the basil and garlic for 2 minutes. Add the tomatoes and tomato purée, and cook gently for about 30 minutes, until thickened.

2 Cook the spaghetti according to pack instructions. Meanwhile, turn the grill to high. Add the prawns to the sauce, sprinkle over the cheeses to cover, then slide the pan under the grill for 6 minutes, until the cheese is golden and bubbling and the prawns have turned pink. Serve with the pasta and scattered with basil leaves, if you like.

More clever ideas using prawns and pasta

■ **Chilli prawn linguine** Mix 2 tbsp virtually fat-free fromage frais with the grated rind and juice of 2 limes and 2 tsp caster sugar. Season. Cook the pasta according to pack instructions, adding 200g trimmed sugar snap peas for the last 2 minutes of cooking time. Meanwhile, heat 2 tbsp olive oil in a frying pan, add 2 chopped garlic cloves, and 1 large red chilli, deseeded and finely chopped, and cook for 30 seconds. Tip in 24 raw, peeled, king prawns and cook over a high heat for 3 minutes, until they turn pink. Add 12 halved cherry tomatoes and cook for 3 minutes. Drain the pasta, toss with the prawns and the dressing, then stir in some basil leaves.

■ **Prawn and avocado pasta salad** Cook 400g penne according to pack instructions. Add 400g raw, defrosted, peeled, tiger prawns 2 minutes before the end of cooking time. Drain, cool under cold water, drain again, and transfer to a serving bowl. Mix together 4 tbsp olive oil, the juice and finely grated rind of 1 lemon, 1 chopped garlic clove, 1 avocado, cubed, 250g halved cherry tomatoes, and 2 thinly sliced spring onions, season, then stir into the pasta with 100g rocket and some torn basil leaves.

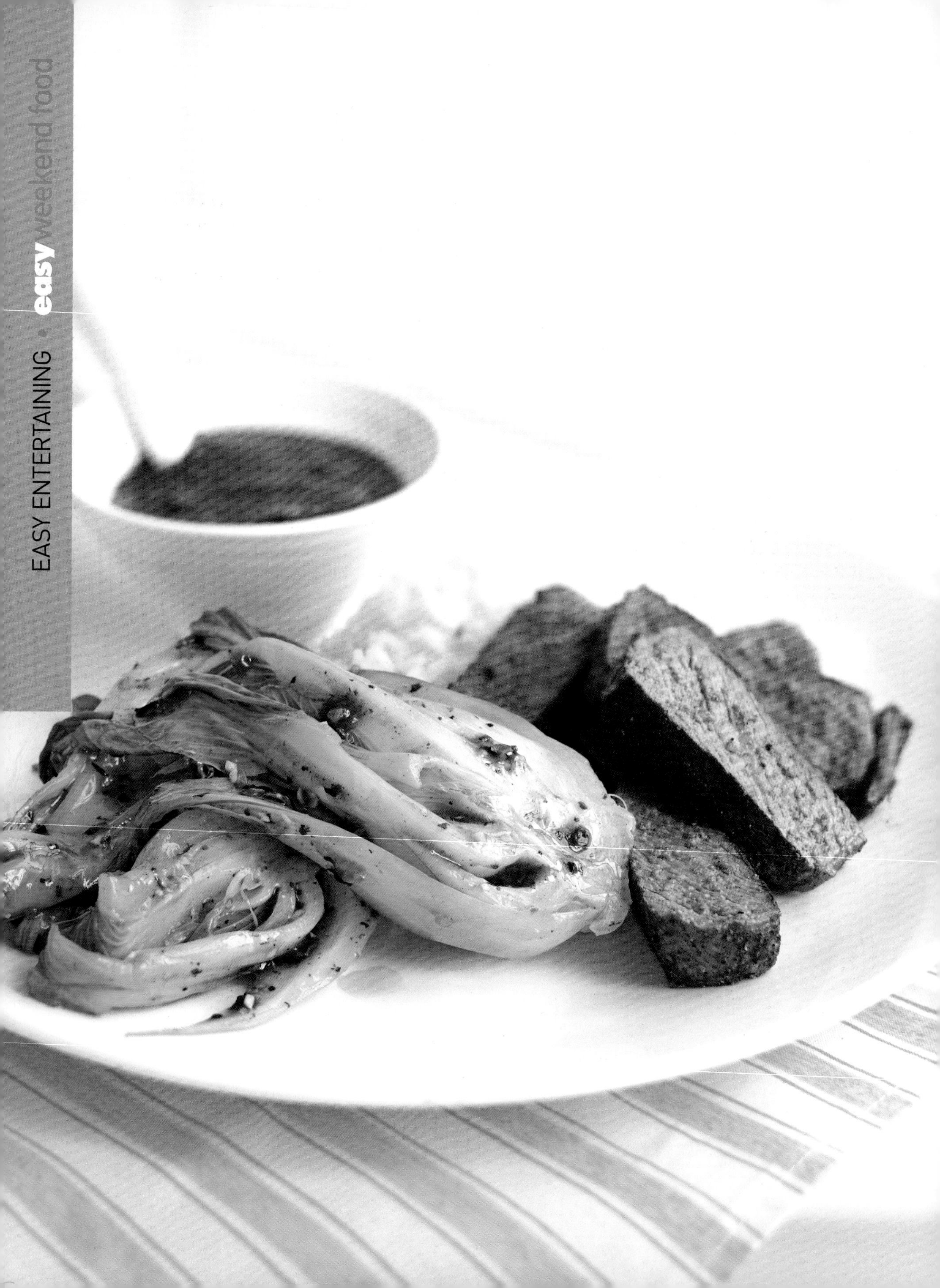

Five-spice beef with black bean sauce

Five-spice powder (a mix of cloves, cinnamon, fennel seeds, star anise and pepper) has a great affinity with beef and we use it a lot in *Easy Cook* recipes (it goes well with stir-fried pork dishes too). We've used bok choi here, but any wilted greens taste extra good if you add a drizzle of sesame oil.

- Serves 2
- Ready in 15 minutes
- Not suitable for freezing

100g sachet black bean sauce
2 cloves of garlic, finely chopped
small knob of ginger, finely grated
2 tbsp rice wine vinegar
2 tsp Chinese five-spice powder
1 large sirloin steak, about 300g
3 heads bok choi, halved
1 tsp sesame oil

1 Mix the black bean sauce, garlic, ginger and rice wine vinegar together in a small pan, then gently simmer until hot.

2 Heat a griddle pan until very hot. Rub the five-spice all over the steak, then season with a little salt and pepper. Sear the steak for 2-3 minutes on each side until cooked to your liking, then leave to rest.

3 Meanwhile, gently simmer or steam the bok choi for 4–5 minutes until wilted, but still crunchy. Toss the greens in a few tablespoons of sauce and the sesame oil. Cut the steak into thick slices. Serve on a plate with a small pot of the remaining sauce and the greens.

Serve with rice.

Pea, tarragon and cream cheese pithiviers

Even if you eat meat, you'll love these tasty veggie pies. They can be assembled up to a day ahead, then covered with cling film and chilled until ready to bake.

- Serves 4
- Ready in 45 minutes
- Not suitable for freezing

1 onion, finely chopped
knob of butter
150g frozen peas, defrosted
125g full-fat soft cheese
1 tbsp chopped tarragon
grated rind of ½ lemon
handful flat-leaf parsley, chopped
500g pack puff pastry
a little flour
1 egg, beaten

1 Cook the onion in the butter for 10 minutes, until very soft. Put in a bowl and add the peas, soft cheese, tarragon, lemon rind and parsley. Mix together with plenty of seasoning.

2 Turn the oven to fan 180C/conventional 200C/gas 6. Thinly roll out the pastry on a lightly floured surface, then cut out 4 circles using a saucer as a template and 4 slightly bigger circles. Divide the filling among the smaller circles, brush around the edges with some of the egg and lay the bigger circles on top. Press the edges together with the prongs of a fork, score a pattern on the top and brush with more egg. Bake for 25 minutes, until golden.

Serve with salad.

Pan-fried pork with crème fraîche and prunes

Prunes may seem an unlikely ingredient here, but they add a rich depth of flavour to the mustardy sauce – do try this recipe and you'll see what we mean!

▦ Serves 4
▦ Ready in 20 minutes
▦ Not suitable for freezing

2 pork fillets, thickly sliced into medallions
2 tbsp plain flour, seasoned
25g butter
20 ready-to-eat pitted prunes
2 tbsp brandy
300ml white wine
1 tbsp dijon mustard
1 tbsp redcurrant jelly
200ml tub crème fraiche

1 Dust the pork with a little of the seasoned flour. Heat the butter in a large non-stick frying pan, then cook the pork in batches for about 3 minutes on each side.

2 Remove from the pan, then add the prunes, brandy, wine, mustard and redcurrant jelly, and simmer to reduce the mixture by half.

3 Stir in the crème fraiche to make a creamy sauce, season well, then return the pork to the pan and heat everything through.

Serve with tagliatelle and broccoli or a green salad.

See photo on page 116

Poached salmon with green herbs and mustard sauce

This is a classic *Easy Cook* recipe – it's really simple, but it looks good and tastes divine. Poaching the salmon keeps it moist and soft, and the sauce takes just minutes to whizz together.

▦ Serves 2 (easily multiplied)
▦ Ready in 20 minutes
▦ Not suitable for freezing

2 skinless salmon fillets
2 tbsp chopped tarragon
2 tbsp chopped flat-leaf parsley
2 tsp dijon mustard
2 tbsp white wine vinegar
2 tbsp olive oil

1 Bring a shallow pan of water to a simmer. Put in the salmon, put a lid on the pan and cook for 5–6 minutes. Lift the salmon out with a slotted spoon.

2 Put all the other ingredients in a small food processor and whizz until smooth (if it's too thick, add a splash of water).

Serve the salmon drizzled with the sauce, with potatoes and watercress.

Baked peaches with rose water

You'll find rose water in larger supermarkets, either in the baking section or with the ethnic ingredients.

- Serves 6
- Ready in 25 minutes
- Not suitable for freezing

6 ripe peaches, halved and stoned
juice of 1 large orange
2 tbsp rose water
100g caster sugar
2 cinnamon sticks, broken

1 Turn the oven to fan 200C/conventional 220C/gas 7. Put the peaches cut-side-up in a shallow heatproof dish so they fit snugly. Mix the orange juice with the rose water, pour over the peaches, then scatter with the sugar.

2 Scatter over the cinnamon sticks and bake for 20 minutes, until the peaches are tender. Serve warm or chilled.

Serve with yogurt or ice cream and a sprig of mint.

Plum kulfis

This is a really good dessert to serve after spicy or strong-flavoured food (such as a curry). Make sure the plums are really soft at the end of step 1 so that they whizz easily into a nice, smooth purée.

- Serves 6
- Ready in 30 minutes, plus freezing
- Suitable for freezing

3 cardamom pods
700g plums, halved and stoned
100g caster sugar
400ml can condensed milk
150ml milk
2 tbsp chopped pistachio nuts

1 Split the cardamom pods and remove the seeds, then crush the seeds with a pestle and mortar, or the end of a rolling pin in a cup. Put in a pan with the plums, sugar and 5 tbsp water, then bring to the boil. Reduce the heat, cover, then cook for 10 minutes until the plums are very soft. Tip into a food processor and blend until smooth. Pour into a jug and leave to cool.

2 Mix together the condensed milk, the ordinary milk and 300ml of the plum purée. Pour into 6 ramekins, plastic beakers or small cups, then freeze for 4 hours, or until firm.

3 To serve, dip each mould briefly into hot water, then invert them onto small plates. Pour a little plum purée around each kulfi and sprinkle with chopped pistachios.

Strawberry vanilla tart

Look out for ready-made sweet shortcrust pastry in the chiller cabinet at the supermarket – it works better in a tart like this than standard shortcrust. The pastry case needs to be 'blind baked' (as in step 1) without the filling to ensure it stays crisp. If you don't have any baking beans for this, use dried lentils or dried pasta instead.

- Serves 8
- Ready in 40 minutes
- Not suitable for freezing

250g sweet shortcrust pastry
5 egg yolks
2 tsp vanilla sugar
100g caster sugar
50g plain flour
425ml milk
25g butter
500g strawberries
2 tbsp redcurrant or quince jelly

1 Turn the oven to fan 170C/conventional 190C/gas 5. Roll out the pastry fairly thinly and use to line a 23cm round shallow tart tin. Line the pastry with a circle of baking parchment and a layer of baking beans. Bake blind for 10 minutes, then lift out the paper and beans, and bake for a further 5 minutes, until the pastry is crisp and golden. Remove from the tin and cool on a wire rack.

2 Meanwhile, whisk together the egg yolks, the vanilla sugar and caster sugar, until the mixture is pale and thick. Whisk in the flour. Heat the milk until just boiling, then gradually whisk into the egg mixture. Pour into a pan and cook over a gentle heat, whisking until the custard is thick and glossy. Cook gently for a further 2 minutes, to take away the raw taste of the flour. Remove from the heat and beat in the butter. Spoon into a clean bowl, cover closely with cling film and leave to cool.

3 Set the pastry case on a flat serving plate. Spread the cool custard over the pastry case almost to fill it (if you have some left over, it freezes well to use another time). Halve the strawberries and arrange in overlapping circles over the custard. Use the largest strawberries for the outer circles and the smallest ones for the centre.

4 Warm the jelly in a pan with 1 tbsp water and brush over the strawberries to glaze them.

Serve with a dusting of icing sugar.

Vanilla yogurt ice

Light, delicious and refreshing – and it looks really pretty too. You don't need an ice-cream machine to make this, but be sure to stir it regularly while it's in the freezer so that no large ice crystals form or they will spoil the texture.

- Serves 6
- Ready in 25 minutes, plus freezing
- Suitable for freezing

200g caster sugar
1 vanilla pod, seeds scraped out
two 500g tubs natural yogurt
3 pink grapefruit
4 tbsp clear honey
mint leaves, to scatter

1 Put the caster sugar in a bowl, then rub in the vanilla seeds with your fingers so they're evenly mixed. Stir in the yogurt until the sugar has dissolved. Churn the mixture in an ice-cream machine until frozen, but still soft, or, if you don't have a machine, pour the yogurt into a freezer-safe container and freeze for 4–6 hours, stirring thoroughly every hour or so. Meanwhile, line a 1kg loaf tin with cling film.

2 Spoon the soft frozen yogurt into the tin, cover with another piece of cling film, then freeze for at least 4 hours, until firm. Segment the grapefruit, catching the juices in a bowl – you should get about 200ml. Put the juice into a small pan with the honey, simmer for 10–15 minutes until thickened and syrupy, stir in the grapefruit segments, then leave to cool.

3 Take the yogurt ice from the freezer about 10 minutes before you want to serve it. Cut into slices and serve topped with grapefruit, some of the honeyed sauce and a scattering of mint leaves.

Sorbet fizz

An easy way to jazz up shop-bought sorbet – we've used raspberry sorbet, but any fruit flavour would work well in this recipe. For a more grown-up pud, replace the sparkling elderflower with champagne, cava or prosecco.

- Serves 2
- Ready in 5 minutes
- Not suitable for freezing

2 strawberries, sliced
4 scoops raspberry sorbet
100ml sparkling elderflower water

1 Arrange the strawberry slices in the bottom of 2 tall glasses, then top each with 2 scoops of raspberry sorbet. Pour over the elderflower water and serve straight away.

Lemon and whisky crème caramels

A classic dessert given a contemporary twist with the sharpness of lemon and the sophisticated addition of a splash of whisky. When you add the whisky in step 2, be sure to turn the pan away from you as the caramel will splutter. If the caramels don't tip out easily at the end, dip the bottom of each ramekin into hot water for 5–10 seconds and they will slip out smoothly.

- Serves 6
- Ready in 55 minutes, plus infusing and cooling time
- Not suitable for freezing

700ml whole milk
1 vanilla pod, split in half
4 strips lemon rind
170g caster sugar
50ml whisky
4 whole eggs, plus 4 egg yolks

1 Put the milk, vanilla pod and lemon rind in a pan, and bring to a gentle simmer. Take off the heat, cover and let the flavours infuse for at least 30 minutes before using. Turn the oven to fan 130C/conventional 150C/gas 2.

2 Put 120g of the sugar and half the whisky in a pan. Heat gently until the sugar melts, then turn up the heat and boil, without stirring, until the liquid turns a dark caramel colour. Carefully add the remaining whisky (it will splutter). Heat the caramel through again to remove any lumps and quickly pour it into 6 large, warmed ramekins, turning them as you pour, so the caramel covers the sides and bottoms (don't worry if it hardens).

3 Beat the eggs and egg yolks with the remaining 50g sugar. Scrape the vanilla seeds into the infused milk (remove the pod and lemon rind first) and reheat it until it's hot, but not simmering. Whisk the milk into the eggs and pour into the ramekins.

4 Cover each ramekin with foil. Stand in a roasting tray and pour in water until it reaches one third of the way up the outside of the ramekins. Bake for 35 minutes. Allow to cool, then chill if eating later. Gently run a knife around the sides before turning the caramels out onto a plate.

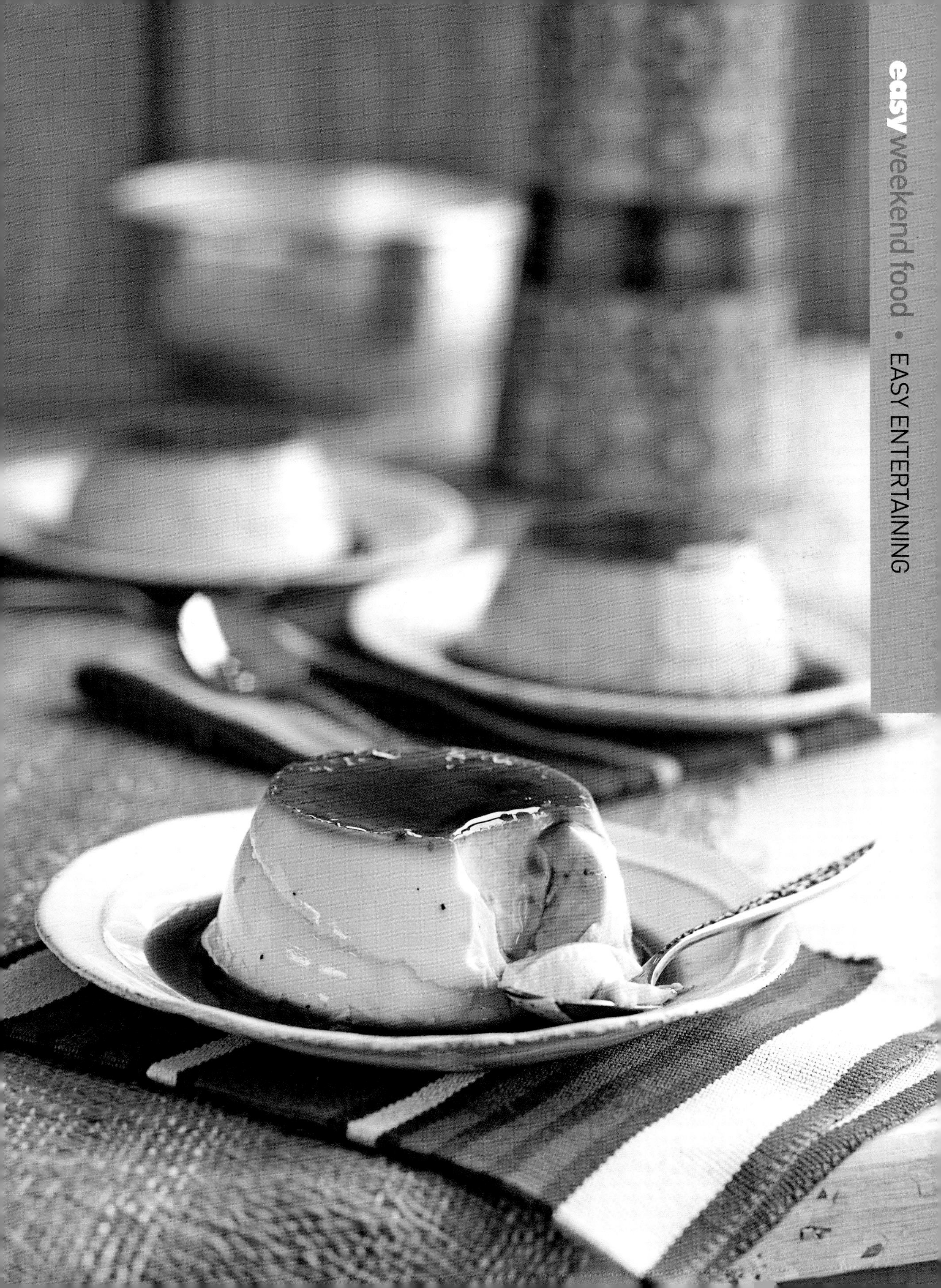

easy
OCCASIONS
It's time to celebrate in style!

Whatever the occasion, cooking something special is a great way to make it memorable.

Baking a birthday cake for someone is the ultimate way to let them know they're special to you, and our chocolate cake recipe over the page is guaranteed to become a firm favourite with both kids and adults. You can change the decoration to suit the birthday girl or boy; we've used candles, but chocolate curls, sprinkles, or a piped message would all work well.

Having a party? Rustle up our *Spicy prawn poppadums* or our *Stilton and poppy seed sables* (a rich, savoury biscuit) to hand round with drinks, or serve our two wonderful desserts as part of a buffet.

And, at Easter, why not make your own hot cross buns? It's easier than you might think and the taste is a million miles away from anything you can buy in the shops.

Christmas is all about the food, and we've got a turkey recipe that will banish any memories of dry, tasteless meat for ever, as well as a clever new take on mince pies, plus *Christmas pud cupcakes* that look great piled up on a cake stand as a table centrepiece. If you want to make a gift for a friend, we recommend our *Christmas biscotti* too.

Chunky mince pie slices, page 143

Chocolate birthday cake

It's simple to add colour to a cake with candles rather than using artificially coloured icing and sweets. If you feel piping the chocolate is too fiddly, you can drizzle it over instead.

■ Serves 12
■ Ready in 45 minutes
■ Suitable for freezing

140g butter, plus extra for the tin
175g caster sugar
2 eggs
225g self-raising flour
50g cocoa powder
¼ tsp bicarbonate of soda
250g natural yogurt
TO DECORATE
300g icing sugar, sieved
2 tbsp cocoa powder, sieved
1 tbsp butter, melted
3–4 tbsp boiling water
50g each milk, plain and white chocolate, broken into squares

1 Turn the oven to fan 160C/conventional 180C/gas 4. Butter and line the base of an 18x28cm cake tin. Put the butter and sugar into a bowl and beat together with electric hand beaters until light and fluffy. Add the eggs a little at a time, beating well.

2 Sieve the flour, cocoa and bicarbonate of soda into the bowl. Pour in the natural yogurt. Stir everything to a smooth mixture and spoon into the prepared tin. Bake for 20–25 minutes until just firm and shrinking away from the sides of the tin. Cool in the tin for 5 minutes, turn onto a wire rack to cool completely.

3 Sieve the icing sugar and cocoa into a bowl, then pour in the butter and 2 tbsp just-boiled water. Stir together until you get a spreadable consistency. If it's too stiff, very carefully add a little more boiling water, drop by drop. Spread the icing over the top of the cake.

4 Melt the chocolates in 3 different bowls in the microwave on High (100%) for 1 minute or over a pan of simmering water. Spoon the melted chocolates into 3 plastic disposable piping bags. Snip the ends off and pipe 12 shapes (we made hearts and spirals) on top of the cake. Leave to set. Just before serving, cut the cake into 12 squares and push in the candles.

Richly fruited hot cross buns

These are made with a bread mix – so there's no messing about with yeast or special flours – but do make sure you buy a bread *mix* (as it contains yeast), rather than bread flour, otherwise the buns won't rise. If you don't have a piping bag for the crosses, use a freezer bag – just snip off the corner.

▓ Makes 12
▓ Ready in 50 minutes, plus rising time
▓ Not suitable for freezing

500g pack white bread mix
50g caster sugar
1 tbsp mixed spice
85g butter
250ml milk
1 egg, beaten
250g bag mixed fruit (including peel)
100g plain flour (for the crosses), plus extra
for rolling
2 tbsp golden syrup or honey, to glaze

1 Tip the bread mix into a bowl, mix in the sugar and spice, and make a well. Melt the butter in a pan, stir in the milk and pour into the well, along with the egg. Use a knife to stir the dry ingredients into the wet to form a dough. Tip onto a work surface and knead for 5 minutes, until smooth. Transfer to a lightly oiled bowl, cover with oiled cling film, and leave to rise in a warm place for 30 minutes, or until twice its size.

2 Turn the dough onto a lightly floured surface and punch the air out. Press the dough out into a large rectangle (about A3 size) and sprinkle over the fruit. Roll the dough up around the fruit and knead until the fruit is evenly dispersed through the dough.

3 Split into 12 even pieces and shape into smooth balls. Grease a large baking sheet and sit the shaped buns on it about 2–3 cm apart, so they have room to rise. Re-cover with the oiled cling film and set aside again in a warm place until they have risen and the dough feels pillowy when prodded gently. Turn the oven to fan 180C/ conventional 200C/gas 6.

4 In a bowl, make a well in the flour and gradually stir in 6 tbsp water (or milk) to make a smooth, pipeable paste. Spoon it into a piping bag and pipe a cross on the buns. Bake for 15–20 minutes, until well risen and golden. Leave to cool for a few minutes, then lift onto a rack. Heat the syrup or honey in a small pan until melted. Brush over the warm buns and leave to cool.

Spicy prawn poppadums

These take just minutes to prepare – which is just as well, because they'll be wolfed down in seconds, as they're always very popular at parties!

■ Makes 24
■ Ready in 10–15 minutes
■ Not suitable for freezing

24 cooked and peeled extra-large tiger prawns, thawed if frozen
24 ready-to-eat mini poppadums, plain or assorted
200g tub tzatziki
a little chopped fresh coriander
paprika, for dusting

1 Dry the prawns on kitchen paper and keep covered in the fridge. Lay out the poppadums on a serving platter.

2 When ready to serve, spoon a little tzatziki into each poppadum. Stand a prawn on top, then finish with a scattering of coriander and a light dusting of paprika.

Stilton and poppy seed sables

You can prepare the dough in advance, but don't assemble the biscuits until just before you want to serve them as they soften if left to stand.

■ Makes about 30 biscuits
■ Ready in 30 minutes, plus chilling time
■ Suitable for freezing

100g plain flour, plus extra for rolling
85g cold butter, diced
small pinch of mustard powder
small pinch of cayenne pepper
1 tbsp polenta (optional)
1 tbsp poppy seeds
100g Stilton, crumbled, plus extra to top the biscuits

1 In a large bowl, rub the flour, butter, mustard powder, cayenne, polenta (if using), poppy seeds, cheese and a pinch of salt together, until it forms a dough. Knead briefly until it sticks together and is lightly speckled with small bits of cheese.

2 On a lightly floured surface, roll the dough with your hands into a sausage shape, about 25cm long and 4cm in diameter. Wrap in cling film and chill for at least 1 hour.

3 To bake the biscuits, turn the oven to fan 170C/conventional 190C/gas 5. Slice the dough into rounds just under 1cm thick. Lay the rounds, evenly spaced, on 2 baking sheets (or cook in batches). Put a very small piece of Stilton in the middle of each biscuit, then bake for 10–15 minutes, until the biscuits are starting to turn golden around the edges and the cheese in the middle is bubbling. Let the biscuits cool slightly before serving.

Skewered melon and prosciutto

A party version of an ever-popular starter dish. To check the melon is ripe before you buy it, give it a sniff – it should have a pleasantly sweet smell at the stalk end. The skewers can be made in advance and kept in the fridge for up to 3 hours.

- Makes 20
- Ready in 15 minutes
- Not suitable for freezing

½ ripe cantaloupe melon, quartered and peeled
6–8 slices prosciutto
20 cocktail sticks

1 Cut the melon into about 20 bite-sized chunks. Cut each prosciutto slice into 3 long strips. Wrap a strip of prosciutto around each melon chunk and secure with a cocktail stick, to serve.

Chunky mince pie slices

You can freeze these, uncooked, on the baking tray for up to 1 month. Defrost overnight and bake.

- Makes 15 slices
- Ready in 35 minutes
- Suitable for freezing

280g mincemeat
25g pecan nuts, mixture of broken and whole
25g pistachio nuts, halved lengthways
2 tbsp flaked almonds
25g dried cranberries
½ small apple, cored and finely chopped
finely grated rind of 1 lemon, plus 2 tsp juice
375g ready-rolled sheet puff pastry
1 rounded tbsp ground almonds
beaten egg, to glaze (optional)
50g icing sugar

1 Turn the oven to fan 200C/conventional 220C/gas 7. First mix the fruit and nut ingredients and the lemon rind.

2 Lay the pastry on a floured work surface. Slice off a strip from one end to leave a 23cm square. From the strip, cut out 15 star shapes, re-rolling the trimmings as necessary. Lay the pastry square on a baking sheet and scatter over the ground almonds. Spread the mincemeat mixture to the edge of the pastry. Lay the stars in lines across the mincemeat, so you can cut out 15 slices when baked. Brush the stars with egg to glaze, if you like.

3 Bake for 15 minutes, or until the pastry's golden. Leave to cool. Mix the icing sugar with 2 tsp of the lemon juice. Drizzle over before cutting into 15 slices.

See photo on page 136

Classic roast turkey with red wine baste

Banish dry turkey meat for ever – this recipe will ensure it's moist and succulent. To save time and hassle on the day, you can stuff and baste the turkey the day before, then put the foil parcel in the fridge overnight. Remove from the fridge about 30 minutes before cooking to bring to room temperature.

- Serves 8-10 with leftovers
- Ready in 3½–4 hours
- Not suitable for freezing

FOR THE STUFFING
1 onion, chopped
50g butter
140g button mushrooms, thickly sliced
200g vacuum-pack whole cooked chestnuts, halved
170g pack Ardennes pâté, cubed
25g pack parsley, chopped
1 tbsp thyme leaves
6 rashers smoked streaky bacon, each rasher cut into 6–8 pieces
140g oatmeal breadcrumbs or white breadcrumbs
2 eggs

1 onion, quartered
fresh or dried bay leaves, to flavour and garnish
4.5–5.6kg bronze turkey, giblets removed
85g butter, softened
1 whole nutmeg
10 rashers streaky bacon
glass of red wine

1 Fry the onion for the stuffing in the butter for 5 minutes. Add the mushrooms, then fry for 5 minutes more. Tip into a bowl. Stir in the remaining stuffing ingredients. Season well. Set aside.

2 Turn the oven to fan 170C/conventional 190C/gas 5. Put the onion and several bay leaves in the cavity between the legs (drumsticks). Now pack half the stuffing into the neck end, pushing it towards the breast. Secure the neck skin in position with skewers and tie the turkey legs together at the top of the drumsticks to give a neat shape. Weigh the turkey and calculate the cooking time at 20 minutes per kilo, plus 90 minutes. (You may need to use your bathroom scales.)

3 Put a large sheet of extra-wide foil in a large roasting tin, then put the turkey on top. Smear the breast with the butter, grate over half the nutmeg and season well. Cover the breast with the bacon, pour over the wine, then loosely bring up the foil and seal well to make a parcel.

4 Roast in the oven, then 90 minutes before the end of cooking time, open the foil, discard the bacon, and drain off the excess fat from the tin. Leaving the foil open, return the turkey to the oven to brown, basting with the juices several times. With the remaining stuffing mix, make stuffing balls. Then, 35 minutes before the end of cooking, put the stuffing balls around the turkey, or cook in a separate, lightly oiled tin.

5 Push a skewer into the thickest part of the thigh – the juices should run clear. If they are pinkish, cook for 15 minutes more, then test again. Transfer the turkey and stuffing balls to a platter, cover with foil and 2 tea towels, and rest for up to 30 minutes before carving. Garnish with more bay leaves.

Christmas pud cupcakes

These little cakes make a great alternative to a traditional festive fruit cake. To make them ahead, freeze the cooled cakes in plastic bags for up to a month.

▧ Makes 12
▧ Ready in 40 minutes
▧ Suitable for freezing (un-iced)

50g dark chocolate, in chunks
140g butter, plus extra for greasing
100ml soured cream
3 eggs, lightly beaten
140g self-raising flour
140g caster sugar
100g ground almonds
6 tbsp cocoa powder
1 tsp baking powder
85g dried sour cherries, plus a few extra
    to decorate
250g icing sugar, sifted
1 tsp custard powder, sifted
12 small bay leaves

1 Turn the oven to fan 170C/conventional 190C/gas 5. Put a 12-hole silicone muffin tray on a baking sheet or butter a non-stick 12-hole muffin tin, and put two criss-crossing strips of baking parchment in each hole.

2 Melt the chocolate and butter over a low heat. Cool a little, then stir in the soured cream and the eggs. Mix the flour, sugar, almonds, cocoa and baking powder in a bowl. Pour in the chocolate mix, stir until smooth, then stir in the cherries. Spoon into the muffin holes so they are three quarters full, then bake for 20 minutes. Cool in the tins.

3 To decorate, mix the icing sugar and custard powder with 2 tbsp water to make a thick icing. Remove the muffins from the tins and cool on a rack. Cut off any rounded tops, stand upside down on the rack, then spoon over the icing. Leave to set, then top with bay leaves and cherries. Best eaten on the day.

Christmas biscotti

Proper Italian biscotti are quite dry as they're often eaten with a cup of coffee after dinner, but this version, which has extra fruit, is great to nibble on at any time.

- Makes about 70
- Ready in 45 minutes, plus cooling time
- Suitable for freezing (part-baked and sliced)

350g plain flour, plus extra for rolling
2 tsp baking powder
2 tsp mixed spice
250g golden caster sugar
3 eggs, beaten
coarsely grated rind of 1 orange
85g raisins
85g dried cherries
50g blanched almonds
50g shelled pistachio nuts

1 Turn the oven to fan 160C/conventional 180C/gas 4. Line 2 baking sheets with baking paper. Put the flour, baking powder, spice and sugar in a large bowl, then mix well. Stir in the eggs and orange rind until the mixture starts forming clumps, then bring the dough together with your hands – it will seem dry at first, but keep kneading until no floury patches remain. Stir in the fruit and nuts until evenly distributed.

2 Turn the dough out onto a lightly floured surface and divide into 4 pieces. With lightly floured hands, roll each piece into a log shape, about 30cm long. Put 2 on each baking sheet, well spaced apart. Bake for 25–30 minutes, until the dough has risen and spread and feels firm. It should still look pale. Remove from the oven, transfer to a wire rack for a few minutes until cool enough to handle, then turn down the oven to fan 120C/conventional 140C/gas 1.

3 Using a serrated bread knife, cut into slices about 1cm thick on the diagonal, then lay the slices flat on the baking sheets. The biscuits can be cooled and frozen flat on the sheet at this point, then bagged and frozen for up to 2 months. Bake for 15 minutes more (20 minutes from frozen), turn over, then bake again for another 15 minutes, until dry and golden. Put onto a wire rack to cool completely. They'll keep for up to a month in an airtight tin, or pack into boxes to give as gifts straight away.

Rhubarb, apple and ginger crunch trifle

Don't waste the syrup from the ginger jar – it's wonderful drizzled over vanilla ice cream. You can prepare the oatmeal and cook the fruit the day before and then assemble the trifle just before you're ready to serve it.

▨ Serves 8
▨ Ready in 30 minutes
▨ Not suitable for freezing

85g coarse oatmeal
1 tsp ground ginger
100g caster sugar, plus extra to taste
3 Bramley apples, peeled, cored and sliced
    into 2cm wedges
2 balls stem ginger in syrup, finely chopped
700g pink rhubarb, trimmed and cut into
    thumb-length pieces
450ml double cream
600ml tub ready-made vanilla custard
approx 300g ginger cake (shop-bought),
    thickly sliced
1 tbsp ginger wine

1 Heat the oatmeal, ground ginger and half the sugar in a non-stick frying pan until the sugar starts to caramelise and the oatmeal begins to colour, stirring often. Tip onto non-stick baking paper to cool, then break into crumbly nuggets.

2 Put the apples in a large pan, then add half the chopped ginger, 50ml water and the remaining caster sugar. Bring to a simmer, then gently cook for about 7 minutes, adding the rhubarb halfway through, until both are softened, but not mushy. Add more sugar to taste, if you like, then leave to cool.

3 Lightly whip the cream and fold half into the custard. Line the base of a large serving bowl with the ginger cake, sprinkle over the wine, then spoon over the fruit, draining off any excess juice. Add a layer of the oatmeal, cover with the custard, then finish with the remaining cream, remaining ginger and oatmeal. (This is best assembled shortly before serving.)

Chocolate orange truffle cake

Orange liqueur and orange-flavoured chocolate give exactly the right balance of flavours here. Lining the loaf tin with cling film first means the cake will come out easily when you're ready to serve it. It can be frozen for up to a month.

- Serves 10
- Ready in 45 minutes, plus freezing time
- Suitable for freezing

1 orange
5 tbsp orange liqueur
50g caster sugar
350g orange dark chocolate (two chocolate oranges are ideal), broken into pieces
85g unsalted butter, softened
3 eggs, separated
300ml tub double cream, plus extra whipped cream for serving
140g rich tea fingers

1 Line the base and sides of a 1kg loaf tin with cling film. Squeeze the juice from the orange and mix with 3 tbsp of the orange liqueur then set aside. Cut away the bitter white pith from inside the orange shell, then cut the peel into fine strips and boil it in a covered pan with 300ml water for 20 minutes, until soft. Add the sugar, then simmer uncovered for a few minutes, until you have a soft, sticky peel.

2 Meanwhile, melt the chocolate over a pan of water, then remove from the heat and beat in the butter and egg yolks, followed by the rest of the liqueur. Whisk the egg whites until they hold their shape, then whip the cream until softly stiff. Fold the egg whites and cream into the chocolate mixture.

3 Spoon 5 large tbsps of the chocolate mixture into the tin, then dip the biscuits in the orange and liqueur mixture and arrange over the chocolate layer – don't soak them too much or they will fall apart. Reserve and freeze about half the sticky peel for the final decoration, then scatter some of the remaining peel over the chocolate layer. Spoon on another 5 tbsp of the chocolate mixture. Carry on layering up the biscuits and chocolate mixture until you have 4 layers of biscuit, finishing with a chocolate layer. Lightly cover with cling film and freeze until ready to serve.

4 To serve, take the cake and orange peel out of the freezer no more than 1 hour before serving and strip off the cling film. Top with the extra whipped cream and the remaining peel, and scatter with grated chocolate, if you like. Keep chilled until ready to eat.

easy
OUTDOOR EATING

Make the most of the summer with an alfresco meal

Whether you're planning to fire up the barbecue or to spread out a picnic rug on the grass, look no further for recipe inspiration.

We've got some delicious main courses that can be cooked over the coals, from spicy *Red curry chicken kebabs* to gloriously *Sticky ribs with corn salad* and of course there's a meat-free option in the form of our wonderful *Veggie burgers*, too. And do try the *Ember-baked potatoes* that can be cooked among the glowing coals and then served with three different flavoured butters. We haven't forgotten pudding, either: put *Hot chocolate bananas* on the dying embers and they'll be ready by the time you've finished your main course. There are some great *Easy Cook* tips for trouble-free barbecuing on page 156 too.

For the perfect picnic, you need food that's easy to transport and easy to serve. Our *Picnic pie* fits the bill perfectly, as does the wonderful *White chocolate and cherry loaf*. We've decorated ours with mascarpone and chocolate curls for a special touch, but it's still lovely without the topping if you'd rather keep things simple.

We've also included a clever 'no cook' recipe for when the weather's so hot that you just want to get out of the kitchen as quickly possible. Our goat's cheese pizza has all the flavours of the classic dish but the base is a focaccia or ciabatta loaf.

Chicken, mushroom and avocado salad, page 162

Ember-baked potatoes with 3 butters

We've used 3 different flavoured butters here – make more than you need as they freeze well to use another time (try them on grilled steaks).

■ Serves 6
■ Ready in 55 minutes

12 small baking potatoes, washed
2–3 tbsp olive oil
a sprinkling of sea salt
CHEDDAR, CHIVE AND TOMATO BUTTER
125g soft butter
75g mature cheddar, finely grated
2 tbsp snipped chives
1 tbsp tomato purée
HERB AND GARLIC BUTTER
125g soft butter
4 tbsp chopped parsley, basil, thyme or dill,
**   or a mixture**
1 clove of garlic, crushed
SWEET RED PEPPER BUTTER
125g soft butter
1 roasted red pepper from a jar, finely
**   chopped**
a few shakes of hot sauce

1 Make a batch of each flavour and season. Spoon onto pieces of cling film, wrap into sausage shapes and chill until needed.

2 Pierce the potatoes several times with a fork. Put into a bowl and coat lightly with olive oil and a sprinkling of sea salt. Wrap each potato in a double layer of foil. As soon as the barbecue coals are glowing red, put the potatoes directly into the coals, using tongs. Cook for about 20 minutes, then turn over, and cook for a further 20 minutes, until they are tender, with a crisp, golden skin.

3 Once the potatoes are cooked, carefully remove the foil, split the potatoes open and serve topped with a slice of flavoured butter.

Top tips for an easy barbecue

■ Allow at least 30–40 minutes between lighting the barbecue and adding your food, to ensure it gets to the right temperature.

■ If using wooden or bamboo skewers, soak them in cold water for about half an hour before cooking – this will help stop them burning.

■ Fish can stick badly to a barbecue grill, so wrap it in foil, or use a special BBQ fish cage or fish grill.

■ Take the meat out of the fridge an hour before you want to cook it.

■ If you're cooking vegetarian options and meat at the same time, buy a disposable BBQ to cook the veggie food on and keep it separate (or cook it in a baking parchment bag).

■ Don't use a fork to turn meat as this will let the juices escape. Instead, invest in some long-handled tongs.

Red curry chicken kebabs

A great way to use up the last couple of spoonfuls in a jar of curry paste – you don't need much of it to pack a punch when you're using it to coat chunks of meat for the barbecue.

- Serves 2 (easily multiplied)
- Ready in 15 minutes
- Not suitable for freezing

2 boneless, skinless chicken breasts, cut into large chunks
2 tbsp Thai red curry paste
2 tbsp coconut milk
1 red pepper, deseeded and cut into chunks
1 courgette, halved and cut into chunks
1 red onion, cut into large chunk

1 Tip the chicken, curry paste and coconut milk into a bowl, then mix well until the chicken is evenly coated.

2 Thread the vegetables and chicken onto skewers. Cook on the barbecue for 7 minutes, until the chicken is cooked.

Serve with herby rice, salad and lemon or lime wedges.

Veggie burgers

Look out for spicy seasoning mixes in the supermarket – Moroccan mixes work particularly well in this recipe. If you can't find pinto beans, you can use kidney beans instead.

- Makes 8 burgers
- Ready in 30 minutes
- Suitable for freezing

2 tbsp olive oil
2 leeks, sliced
200g mushrooms, sliced
2 large carrots, coarsely grated
1 tbsp spicy seasoning
1 tbsp soy sauce
300g pinto beans, drained and rinsed
100g cheddar, grated
4 slices granary bread, torn

1 Heat half the oil in a pan. Tip in the vegetables, seasoning and soy, then cook for 10 minutes until soft. Tip into a food processor with the beans, cheese and bread, season. Pulse to a thick paste.

2 With wet hands, shape the mixture into 8 burgers. (These can be kept in the fridge for 2 days or frozen between greaseproof sheets for up to 2 months.) Heat the remaining oil in a pan and fry for 3 minutes on each side, until crispy.

Serve with toasted buns, salad, ketchup and mayo.

Also see page 66 for *Really easy beefburgers*.

Goat's cheese 'pizza'

When the weather's too hot to turn on the oven, this no-cook idea is great to rustle up for a picnic.

- Serves 4–6
- Ready in 10 minutes
- Not suitable for freezing

1 round focaccia loaf or long ciabatta
200g jar marinated grilled red and yellow
    peppers in olive oil
3 tbsp pesto
85g bag watercress
100g soft goat's cheese
handful of black olives

1 Slice the bread in half so you have 2 round or long bases. Drain the peppers, reserving the oil. Spread 1 tbsp of the pesto over the cut side of each base.

2 Scatter over the peppers and watercress and crumble over the goat's cheese. Mix the remaining 1 tbsp of pesto with 1 tbsp of oil from the peppers and drizzle it over the pizzas. Scatter over the olives. Cut each pizza into wedges or slices, if you like.

Sticky ribs with corn salad

For maximum stickiness, just before serving shake the roasting tin so the ribs are well coated with the sauce. The salad makes a really good accompaniment, with a hint of sweetness from the corn, a kick of heat from the chilli and a real tang from the lime juice.

- Serves 4
- Ready in 25 minutes
- Not suitable for freezing

12 small or 8 larger pork ribs
150ml shop-bought barbecue sauce
340g can sweetcorn, drained
½ cucumber, diced
1 red chilli, deseeded and finely chopped
½ red onion, chopped
juice ½ lime

1 Heat the grill. In a large pan of water, simmer the ribs for 15 minutes. Drain and pat dry. In a large roasting tin, toss the ribs with the sauce, then barbecue or grill for 8–10 minutes, turning halfway, until the ribs are sticky.

2 Meanwhile, mix the remaining ingredients in a large bowl with some seasoning.

Serve with the salad and lime wedges.

Also see page 66 for *Jerk-spiced ribs.*

Chicken, mushroom and avocado salad

Perfect picnic food! Put the vinaigrette in a clean jam jar and take it with you to dress the salad just before serving – it makes a great dressing for all sorts of other salads too.

- Serves 4
- Ready in 10 minutes
- Not suitable for freezing

2 tsp dijon mustard
4 tbsp clear honey, plus 2 tsp extra for the vinaigrette
4 tbsp red wine vinegar
150ml olive oil
250g button mushrooms, sliced
½ iceberg lettuce, shredded
200g cooked chicken, torn into small pieces
1 avocado, halved, stoned, peeled and sliced
4 tbsp mayonnaise

1 Mix together the mustard, 2 tsp of the honey and the vinegar, and then slowly whisk in the olive oil.

2 Mix the mushrooms with the remaining 4 tbsp honey and the vinaigrette. Divide the lettuce among each plate, then spoon over the mushrooms, chicken and avocado slices. Top with a spoonful of mayo. Serve as it is or add olives, cherry tomatoes, strips of ham, chopped egg, chopped basil or mint.

See photo on page 154

Aubergine with garlic and herb dressing

Slices of aubergine are ideal for cooking on the barbecue because they're quite robust and can stand up well to the high heat. (If the weather takes a turn for the worse, though, these are good cooked under the grill too.)

- Serves 4
- Ready in 15 minutes
- Not suitable for freezing

2 aubergines, sliced into rounds
3 tbsp olive oil
2 tbsp red wine vinegar
2 tsp sugar
2 cloves of garlic, thinly sliced
small handful of mint and parsley, roughly chopped

1 Brush the aubergine slices on both sides with a little olive oil, then barbecue or grill until lightly browned on both sides. Remove and arrange, overlapping, on a platter.

2 Heat the red wine vinegar with the sugar in a small pan until it has dissolved, then brush over the aubergine slices. Heat the remaining oil in a frying pan, add the garlic and fry quickly until lightly toasted, then pour the garlic and oil into a small bowl. Just before serving, scatter the garlicky oil and the herbs over the aubergines.

easyweekend food • EASY OUTDOOR EATING

Griddled flatbreads with salsa and artichoke houmous

If you've never made flatbreads before, give these a try. They're so easy and so much lighter and tastier than anything you can buy in the shops. They're ideal to serve with a selection of dips at a picnic.

▓ Makes 16
▓ Ready in 2 hours
▓ Not suitable for freezing

250g strong wholemeal flour
250g strong white flour, plus extra for
  rolling
two 7g sachets easy-blend yeast
1 tsp sugar
2 tbsp olive oil

1 Tip the flours into a food processor. Add the yeast, sugar and 1 tsp salt, then mix well. Pour in 350ml warm water and the oil, then process to a soft dough. Mix for 1 minute, then leave until doubled in size (about 1 hour).

2 Pulse the dough in a food processor a couple of times just to knock out the air, then tip onto a floured surface. Cut the dough in half and roll out one half to a rectangle about 20x40cm. Trim the edges using a large sharp knife, then cut into eight 10cm squares. Line a large tray or 2 baking sheets with non-stick baking paper and arrange the bread rectangles over the tray in one layer. Then repeat with the other half of the dough. Leave in a warm place for about 30 minutes, until the dough is just starting to rise.

3 Put the bread directly onto the BBQ racks and cook for a couple of minutes until they puff up, then flip over and cook on the other side. Tip into a basket and serve with the dips, below.

Red pepper and tomato salsa

▪ Tip 100g quartered cherry tomatoes, 1 clove of garlic and 1 deseeded and chopped green chilli into a food processor. Add 200g roasted red peppers from a jar, 1 torn slice of bread and 1 tbsp red wine vinegar, and season well. Pulse to make a rough purée, spoon into a bowl, cover and chill.

Pea and artichoke houmous

▪ Put 140g frozen peas into a bowl and pour over boiling water to cover. Leave for 5 minutes, then drain well and tip into a food processor with 100g artichoke hearts from a jar, 2 tsp ground cumin, 2 tbsp lemon juice, 4 tbsp olive oil and a small handful of mint leaves. Season well, pulse to make a rough purée, then spoon into a small bowl. Cover and chill until ready to serve.

Spicy falafels

Filling and fast, falafels are really versatile and these make a great picnic dish, with pitta bread spread with houmous or tzatiki and a little salad. Add some diced red chilli to the falafel mixture for extra spice, if you like.

- Makes 6
- Ready in 20 minutes
- Suitable for freezing

2 tbsp sunflower oil
1 small onion, finely chopped
1 clove of garlic, crushed
400g can chickpeas, rinsed and drained
1 tsp ground cumin
1 tsp ground coriander
handful of parsley, chopped
1 egg, beaten

1 Heat 1 tbsp of the oil in a large pan, then fry the onion and garlic over a low heat for 5 minutes until softened. Tip into a large mixing bowl with the chickpeas and spices, then mash together with a fork or potato masher until the chickpeas are totally broken down. Stir in the parsley, with seasoning to taste. Add the egg, then squish the mixture together with your hands.

2 Shape the mix into 6 balls, then flatten into patties. Heat the remaining oil in the pan, then fry the falafels on a medium heat for 3 minutes on each side, until golden brown and firm.

Zesty ginger chicken

Leave the chicken to marinate in the fridge for up to 24 hours, if you can, for extra flavour. Be careful not to have the coals burning too fiercely when you cook the meat or the marinade will burn.

- Serves 4 (easily halved or doubled)
- Ready in 30 minutes
- Not suitable for freezing

4 chicken breasts, skin on
1 tsp black peppercorns
3cm piece root ginger
2 cloves of garlic
1 tbsp soy sauce
grated rind of 1 and juice of 2 limes

1 Slash each chicken breast 3 times and put in a shallow dish. Crush the peppercorns coarsely with a pestle and mortar (or in a cup with the end of a rolling pin). Finely grate the ginger, crush the garlic and mix with the soy sauce, peppercorns, lime rind and juice. Mix well, then pour over the chicken and leave to marinate for at least 10 minutes.

2 Barbecue the chicken for 6–8 minutes, then turn it over and cook for 6–8 minutes more, until cooked through. Transfer to a serving dish, then carefully pour over any remaining cooking juices.

Serve with lime wedges for squeezing over.

Also see page 65 for *Barbecued corn with summery butter*.

Smoky cheese and onion tart

No need to line a tart tin for this recipe – just roll out a rectangle of pastry and fold up the edges to make a rim. You can use any hard cheese for this recipe, in place of the cheddar.

- Makes 6
- Ready in 40 minutes
- Not suitable for freezing

small knob of butter
6 rashers smoked bacon, chopped into pieces
3 onions, thinly sliced
200ml double cream
500g block shortcrust pastry (all-butter has the best flavour)
plain flour, for dusting
140g cheddar, half grated, half crumbled
1 egg, beaten
140g cherry tomatoes, halved

1 Turn the oven to fan 200C/conventional 220C/gas 7. Heat the butter in a frying pan until sizzling, then add the bacon and cook for 6 minutes until just starting to crisp. Add the onions and cook for 10 minutes, until soft, sticky and golden. Pour in the cream, take off the heat and leave to cool a little.

2 Meanwhile, roll the pastry out on a lightly floured surface to a rectangle a little bigger than a sheet of A4 paper and transfer to a non-stick baking tray. Roll the edges up and press down to create a raised border.

3 Tip the bacon, onion and cream mixture into a bowl. Mix in the grated cheddar and most of the beaten egg. Spread the mixture over the pastry, then scatter over the tomatoes and the crumbled cheddar. Brush the borders of the tart with the remaining beaten egg, then bake for 20 minutes, or until golden. Leave to cool, then cut into 6 squares.

Blueberry lemon cake

The ideal cake to pack up and take on a picnic.

- Makes 16 squares
- Ready in 1 hour
- Suitable for freezing

300g soft butter, plus extra for greasing
425g caster sugar
grated rind of 1 lemon
6 eggs
250g self-raising flour
300g blueberries
200g desiccated coconut
200g lemon curd

1 Turn the oven to fan 160C/conventional 180C/gas 4. Grease and line a 20x30cm cake tin with baking parchment. Beat together 250g of the butter with 250g sugar and the lemon rind until light and fluffy. In a separate bowl, beat 4 eggs with a fork, then gradually beat into the butter and sugar mixture, adding a spoonful of flour if it begins to curdle. When the eggs are incorporated, fold in the flour and a third of the blueberries, then spoon into the tin. Flatten the surface with a spatula, sprinkle over another third of the blueberries, and bake for 20 minutes until the surface is set.

2 Melt the rest of the butter, then stir in the coconut, and the remaining sugar and 2 eggs until combined. Warm the lemon curd gently in a small pan until runny and pourable.

3 Scatter the remaining blueberries over the top of the part-baked cake, drizzle over the lemon curd, and crumble over the coconut mixture. Bake for 20–25 minutes more, until golden. Leave in the tin to cool. Cut into 16 squares and store in a tin.

Hot chocolate bananas

These make the most of the dying embers of the barbecue and because the bananas are cooked in their skins, you won't need to wash the grill after you've cooked the meat.

- Serves 4
- Ready in 10 minutes
- Not suitable for freezing

4 bananas
12 cubes dark chocolate

1 Lay the bananas so that they are flat on the work surface. Cut a deep slit down the centre and push in the cubes of chocolate.

2 Put on the barbecue and leave until the chocolate melts and the bananas are starting to bubble. Eat hot straight from the skins.

Picnic pie

This freezes well, so it is great to keep stashed away for a last-minute picnic. Sausagemeat can sometimes be tricky to get hold of so if you can't find any, use sausages instead. Simply slit the skins with a sharp knife and squeeze out the filling – this also give you the opportunity to use different flavourings (pork and apple sausages work really well in the pie).

▧ Serves 6
▧ Ready in 1 hour 15 minutes
▧ Suitable for freezing

butter, for greasing
500g block puff pastry
175g sausagemeat
1 apple, peeled, cored and grated
1 onion, grated
1 tbsp thyme leaves
8 thick slices cooked ham, fat trimmed
2 tbsp dijon mustard
1 egg, beaten to glaze

1 Turn the oven to fan 170C/conventional 190C/gas 5. Butter a 20cm springform tin or a deep, loose-based tart tin. Cut two-thirds of the pastry off the block, then roll it out and use to line the tin, leaving a good amount of excess hanging over the edge. Roll out the remaining pastry and cut out a circle to make the top of the pie.

2 Mix the sausagemeat with the apple, onion and thyme. Line the base of the pie with a third of the ham, spread over a third of the mustard and spoon over a third of the sausagemeat. Press down to level it. Add another layer of ham, mustard and sausagemeat, and repeat with one more layer, finishing with the sausagemeat. Level off the top of the pie.

3 Put the pastry lid on top and brush with beaten egg. Fold the excess pastry over and press gently and trim the edges to neaten. Brush again with beaten egg and cut a steam hole in the centre. Bake for 50 minutes, or until a skewer pushed in through the steam hole comes out very hot. Cool in the tin for 15 minutes, then release the sides of the tin and cool completely on a rack (leave the pie on the tin base). Cut into wedges and serve with pickles and salad. Or slide off the base and wrap tightly in foil, then wrap in cling film and freeze.

White chocolate and cherry loaf

Make the most of fresh cherries with this delicious cake. Slice it before setting off on your picnic and wrap the slices tightly in foil. It's also ideal to take on long car journeys – perfect with a cup of tea from a flask.

▨ Cuts into 12 slices
▨ Ready in 1 hour 30 minutes, plus cooling time
▨ Suitable for freezing (un-iced)

225g butter, softened
225g caster sugar
4 eggs, beaten
2 tsp vanilla extract
225g self-raising flour, sifted, plus extra for dusting
375g fresh cherries, pitted
175g white chocolate, chopped into small chunks, plus 100g in small pieces
140g half-fat mascarpone
white chocolate curls (see below) or fresh cherries, to decorate

1 Turn the oven to fan 160C/conventional 180C/gas 4. Line a 1kg loaf tin with baking parchment, so that the paper comes up higher than the sides. Beat the butter and sugar together until fluffy, then add the eggs, a little at a time, along with the vanilla. Fold in the flour until you have a smooth mixture.

2 Dust the cherries in a little flour, then carefully stir half the fruit and half the chopped chocolate into the mixture. Spoon into the prepared tin, then scatter the remaining cherries and remaining half of the chopped chocolate on top, pressing them in lightly. Bake for 1 hour 10 minutes to 1 hour 15 minutes, or until a skewer inserted into the middle comes out clean. Make sure you don't mistake melted chocolate for raw cake mix. Leave to cool in the tin for a few minutes, then turn out onto a wire rack and leave to cool completely.

3 Remove the mascarpone from the fridge, that that it comes to room temperature. Melt the 100g white chocolate pieces in a bowl over a pan of hot water. Quickly stir in 1 tbsp of the mascarpone, then beat in the rest (don't over-beat, though, or it will become grainy). Spread over the top of the loaf (it doesn't need to be too neat) and finish with white chocolate curls or fresh cherries to decorate.

How to make the chocolate curls

■ Melt 150g white chocolate in a bowl over a pan of hot water. Pour onto a baking sheet and spread into a thin layer. Leave until just set, then put a palette knife at a 45-degree angle to the surface and pull it towards you, so the chocolate curls up. For smaller curls, pull a swivel peeler over the smooth side of a whole block of chocolate.

easy
BAKING

Fill the house with the delicious aroma of homemade bakes

It's arguably the most rewarding kind of cooking: fun to do and with delicious results that you can eat straight away.

For many of us, baking is the kind of cooking we like best. Rather then being a chore that we have to do whether we feel like it or not, it's something that we can choose to do for pleasure.

Classic scones are a good place to start. Serve them with jam and cream (and don't worry about which should go on first – they taste great both ways!), or turn them into a lovely old-fashioned scone-topped pud. If you've never made

bread before, try our *Quick carrot and walnut bread*. It's delicious served with soup on a cold winter's day, as are our *Olive bread swirls*.

There's an easy sponge cake, impressive brownies with a clever way of getting a marbled effect, and even flapjacks that can be made in the microwave in just 10 minutes – since we first came up with this recipe, they've become a real *Easy Cook* favourite.

Marbled chocolate brownies, page 182

Classic scones

Serve these with jam or lemon curd and cream, or turn them into fruit scones by adding 85g chopped sultanas or other dried fruit to the dough.

- Makes 8
- Ready in 25 minutes
- Suitable for freezing

350g self-raising flour, plus extra for dusting
¼ tsp salt
1 tsp baking powder
85g butter, cut into cubes
3 tbsp caster sugar
175ml milk
1 tsp vanilla extract
squeeze of lemon juice
beaten egg, to glaze

1 Turn the oven to fan 200C/conventional 220C/gas 7. Tip the flour into a large bowl with the salt and baking powder, then stir to mix together. Add the butter and rub it into the flour with your fingertips until it looks like fine crumbs. Stir in the sugar.

2 Put the milk into a jug and heat in the microwave for about 30 seconds until warm, but not hot. Add the vanilla and lemon juice, then set aside. Put a baking sheet into the oven.

3 Make a well in the flour mix, then add the milk mixture and combine it quickly with a knife – the dough will seem quite wet at first. Scatter some flour onto the work surface and tip out the dough. Dredge the dough and your hands with a little more flour, then fold the dough over 2–3 times until it's a little smoother. Pat into a round about 4cm deep – don't make it too thin or the scones won't be tall enough once baked.

4 Take a 5cm cutter (smooth-edged cutters tend to cut more cleanly, giving a better rise), dip it into some flour and cut out 4 scones. Press what's left of the dough back into a round to cut out another 4. Brush the tops with beaten egg, then carefully put onto the pre-heated baking tray. Bake for 10 minutes, until risen and golden on top. Eat just warm or cold on the day of baking.

Try this scone-topped pud too...

■ Plum, orange and almond cobbler

Turn the oven to 180C fan/conventional 200C/gas 6. Mix 1.5kg stoned and halved plums, 100g caster sugar, 1 tbsp flour and a stick of cinnamon together in a large baking dish. Add the juice of 2 oranges, cover with foil, then bake for 30 minutes until the fruit has softened. Make the scone dough as above, substituting 50g of the flour for 50g ground almonds. The mixture should be stiff, but spoonable. Remove the plums from the oven, uncover, then top with 6 big spoonfuls of the dough. Scatter with a handful of flaked almonds and a little caster sugar, then bake for 30–35 mins until the topping is golden. Scatter with more caster sugar before serving.

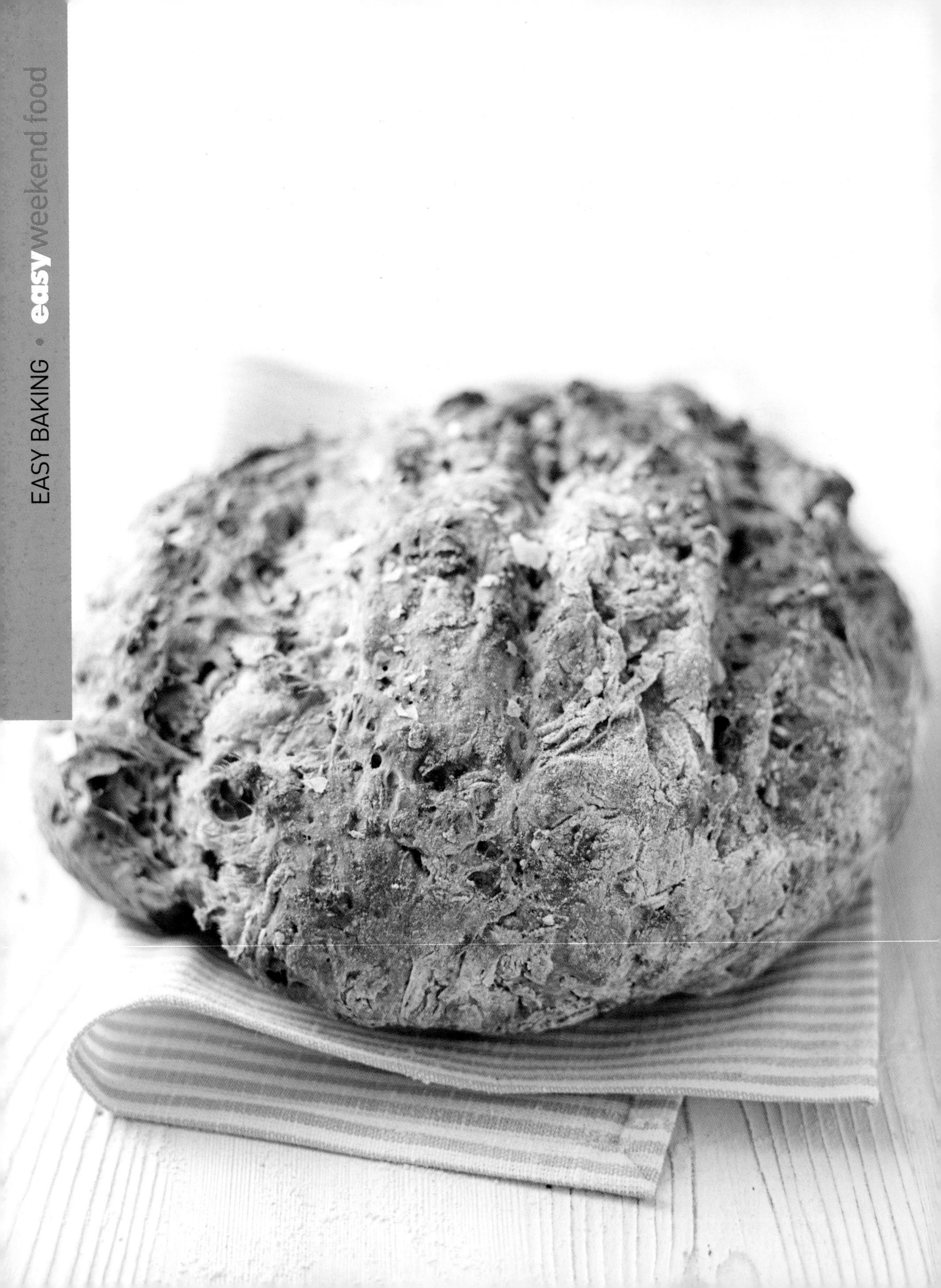

Quick carrot and walnut bread

This speedy-to-make bread needs no time-consuming rising or proving, and is perfect served with soup or topped with cheese and grilled.

- Cuts into 10 slices
- Ready in 50 minutes
- Suitable for freezing

350g plain flour, plus extra for rolling
150g wholemeal flour
1 tsp salt
2 tsp bicarbonate of soda
150g carrots, peeled and grated
handful of walnut pieces, toasted
300g low-fat Greek yogurt
125ml semi-skimmed milk

1 Turn the oven to fan 210C/conventional 230C/gas 8. Mix the flours, salt and bicarbonate of soda, then stir in the carrots, walnuts and yogurt, followed by enough of the milk to make a soft, quite sticky dough.

2 Tip onto a floured surface and form a flat ball, put on a baking sheet, slash the top and bake for 35–40 minutes, until risen and cooked. It should sound hollow underneath when you tap it.

Cheese scone pizza

Add a handful of chopped thyme with the flour in step 1, if you like.

- Serves 4
- Ready in 30 minutes
- Not suitable for freezing

250g plain flour, plus extra for rolling
1 tsp salt
2 tsp baking powder
50g butter, chopped
2 eggs
3 tbsp milk
1 tbsp olive oil
1 green pepper, deseeded and thinly sliced
4 rashers streaky bacon, chopped
5 spring onions, thinly sliced
2 tbsp tomato ketchup
2 tbsp tomato purée
6–8 cherry tomatoes, halved
85g mature cheddar, grated

1 Turn the oven to fan 200C/conventional 220C/gas 7. Mix the flour, salt and baking powder in a bowl, then rub in the butter until the mixture resembles breadcrumbs. Mix the eggs and milk together in a bowl, then stir into the flour and butter mixture to make a soft dough. Use your hands to shape the dough into a round on a lightly floured surface, lift onto a non-stick baking tray, and then press out to a circle, about 24cm wide.

2 Heat the oil in a frying pan, then stir-fry the pepper and bacon until the pepper is soft and the bacon is cooked. Take off the heat, then stir in the spring onion.

3 Mix the ketchup and purée together and spread over the pizza base, then tip over the pepper and bacon mixture. Scatter over the tomatoes, and then the cheese. Bake for 15 minutes, until golden and cooked through.

Marbled chocolate brownies

The marbled effect here looks really impressive but it's easy to create. They will keep in an airtight container for up to 3 days.

▨ Makes 16
▨ Ready in 55 minutes
▨ Suitable for freezing

200g dark chocolate (70% cocoa is best)
200g white chocolate
250g pack unsalted butter, cut into cubes,
   plus extra for greasing
300g caster sugar
4 eggs, beaten
140g plain flour

1 Butter and line a 23cm-square brownie tin and turn the oven to fan 160C/ conventional 180C/gas 4. Put the dark and white chocolate into 2 separate bowls and add half the butter to each. Heat in the microwave, 1 bowl at a time, on full power (100%) for 1½ minutes, stirring halfway, until each of the mixtures have melted (or melt over a pan of simmering water, making sure the water doesn't touch the base of the bowl). Give each bowl of chocolate and butter a final stir.

2 Add 150g sugar and 2 beaten eggs to each bowl, then beat until smooth. Stir 50g of the flour into the dark chocolate mix and 90g of flour into the white mix.

3 Spoon tablespoons of the batter into the tin, alternating dark and white chocolate to make a patchwork of blobs. Once the bottom of the tin is covered, go over the first layer, spooning white on top of the dark blobs and dark on top of the white. For the marbled effect, pull a skewer through the blobs to make feathery swirls.

4 Bake for 35 minutes, or until the middle is just set and the white chocolate patches have a pale golden crust. Leave to cool in the tin then cut into 16 squares.

See photo on page 176

Try these other brownie ideas too

■ Triple chocolate
Follow the method above, but let the batter cool completely at the end of step 2, then add 50g roughly chopped chunks of milk chocolate to each and stir. Continue with steps 3 and 4.

■ Dark chocolate and raspberry
Use the same measurements as in the main recipe, but use 400g dark chocolate (omit the white chocolate), and make the batter in 1 bowl. At the end of step 2, stir in 200g thawed frozen raspberries, spoon into the tin and continue with step 4.

■ Choc-orange marbled brownies
Make the brownies as in the main recipe. While they're cooling, beat together 200g full-fat soft cheese, 1 tsp vanilla extract, the juice of ½ orange and 50g icing sugar until smooth. Spread over each brownie.

Olive bread swirls

These are good with soup or a hunk of cheese for lunch, and they're delicious to serve at a barbecue or on a picnic too.

- Makes 12
- Ready in 45 minutes
- Suitable for freezing

500g strong white flour, plus extra for rolling
1 tsp salt
7g sachet easy-blend dried yeast
5 tbsp extra-virgin olive oil, plus extra for brushing
small bunch of basil
170g pitted black olives
1 clove of garlic, crushed
4 anchovies from a can (optional)
50g pitted green olives

1 In a large bowl, mix the flour, salt, yeast, 1 tbsp olive oil and 300ml warm water, to make a soft dough. Knead by hand for 10 minutes, or with the dough hook in a food processor or mixer for 5 minutes. Put the dough back into a clean mixing bowl, then cover the bowl with oiled cling film. Leave to rise for an hour in a warm place, until doubled in size.

2 Discard any tough basil stalks (leave tender ones on) and put in a mini food processor or hand blender beaker with the black olives. Add the remaining 4 tbsp olive oil, the garlic and the anchovies, if using. Whizz to a rough paste.

3 Turn the oven to fan 200C/conventional 220C/gas 7. Line a shallow baking tin about 30x20cm with non-stick baking paper. On a floured worktop, roll out the dough to a rectangle roughly 30x40cm. Spread the olive paste over the dough and arrange the whole green olives in a line down one of the short edges. Roll up the dough like a Swiss roll, starting at the short olive-encrusted end, to make a sausage shape. Cut the dough into 12 slices, then carefully lift each one into the tin, to make 4 rows of 3 swirl shapes. Lightly brush all over with the extra olive oil. Loosely cover with cling film, then leave to rise for 20–25 minutes, until slightly puffed up and filling the tin. Cook for 20–25 minutes until golden, then leave to cool in the tin until ready to serve.

Classic sponge cake

Ideal for celebrations, or just when you fancy a treat, this recipe is really straightforward. Defrosted frozen berries make a great filling in place of jam too.

- Cuts into 8 slices
- Ready in 40 minutes
- Suitable for freezing (sponge only)

200g soft butter, plus extra for greasing
200g self-raising flour
1 tsp baking powder
250g caster sugar
4 eggs
2 tbsp milk
150ml tub double cream
½ tsp vanilla essence
100g strawberry jam
icing sugar, for dusting

1 Turn the oven to fan 160C/conventional 180C/gas 4. Grease two 20cm round non-stick sandwich tins with butter and line the bases with baking parchment, then lightly grease the parchment. Sift the flour and baking powder into a large bowl, then tip in the butter, 200g of the sugar, the eggs and milk. Using an electric whisk, beat everything together until smooth.

2 Divide the mixture between the cake tins, then bake for 20–25 minutes, until golden. Don't be tempted to open the oven door until 20 minutes is up, or the sponges may sink.

3 Press the top of both cakes – when they're cooked, they will spring back immediately. When cool enough to handle, turn out the cakes from the tins, then leave to cool completely on a wire rack.

4 To make the filling, whip the cream with the remaining 50g caster sugar and vanilla essence until it holds its shape. Assemble the cake by spreading 1 sponge with cream, then the jam. Sandwich the sponges together, then dust with icing sugar to serve.

Try these variations too...

■ Chocolate fudge cake
Substitute 50g of the flour for 50g cocoa powder and sift together with the other dry ingredients. Sandwich the cake with 150g chocolate spread (softened for a few seconds in the microwave if it's too solid) and dust with a little extra cocoa powder to serve.

■ Coffee and walnut cake
Mix 2 tbsp coffee granules with 50ml hot water. Stir half into the cake batter with 50g chopped walnuts. Beat 250g mascarpone with 75g icing sugar and the rest of the coffee mixture. Use half to sandwich the cake and spread the rest over the top.

■ Lemon drizzle cake
Add the grated rind of 1 lemon to the cake mix before baking. Sandwich the cooled cakes with 100g lemon curd. Mix the juice of the lemon with 50g granulated sugar and drizzle over the top of the cake.

Microwave flapjacks

This must be the quickest-ever flapjack recipe – and it's utterly delicious! Don't worry if the mixture still looks quite pale when the cooking time is up – so long as it has started to bubble in the centre, it will darken up as it cools.

- Makes 8
- Ready in 10 minutes
- Suitable for freezing

85g butter
2 tbsp golden syrup
85g soft dark brown sugar
150g porridge oats
50g raisins
85g dried apricots, chopped

1 Put the butter, syrup and sugar into a microwaveable bowl and cook on full power (100%) for 1 minute, until melted. Stir in the remaining ingredients and mix well.

2 Press into a 20cm round, shallow dish lined with greaseproof paper and cook on full power (100%) for 3½ minutes, or until the centre is bubbling. Allow to cool, then cut into wedges.

Mango and passion fruit roulade

The trick here is to roll the sponge up like a Swiss roll as soon as it comes out of the oven.

- Makes 10 slices
- Ready in 30 minutes, plus cooling time
- Suitable for freezing (unfilled sponge only)

3 eggs
85g caster sugar, plus extra for dusting and the filling
85g plain flour, sifted
1 tsp baking powder, sifted
1 tsp vanilla extract
flesh from 2 large, ripe passion fruits
2 mangoes, peeled and cut into small chunks
250g pack frozen raspberries, defrosted
200g tub 2% Greek yogurt or very low-fat fromage frais

1 Turn the oven to fan 180C/conventional 200C/gas 6. Grease and line a 30x24cm swiss roll tin with non-stick baking paper. Put the eggs and sugar into a large bowl and beat for about 5 minutes with an electric whisk, until thick and pale. Fold in the flour and baking powder, then the vanilla extract. Tip into the tin, tilt to level the mix, then bake for 12–15 minutes until golden and just springy. Turn onto another sheet of baking paper, dusted with 1 tbsp caster sugar. Roll the unfilled sponge and keep wrapped in the paper, then leave to cool completely.

2 Fold 1 tbsp of sugar, the passion fruit flesh and one-third of the mango and raspberries into the yogurt. Unroll the sponge, spread the filling over the sponge, then roll it up from the long edge. Serve with the rest of the fruit on the side. The roulade can be filled and rolled up to 2 hours before serving and kept in the fridge.

See photo on pages 90-91

Cheat's raspberry meringue ice cream cake

This looks like a proper cake, but actually there's no real baking involved! It's quick to make but allow enough time for it to freeze – at least 4 hours or, ideally, overnight. It will keep in the freezer for up to 2 weeks.

■ Serves 8
■ Ready in 20 minutes, plus freezing time
■ Suitable for freezing

175g icing sugar
500ml tub fresh custard
500ml tub crème fraiche
2 tsp vanilla extract
oil, for greasing
400g raspberries
100g meringues or meringue nests, broken into small chunks
300g jar raspberry coulis or sauce

1 Reserve 1 tbsp of icing sugar. Mix together the custard, crème fraiche, remaining sugar and vanilla in a large bowl. Put the bowl in the freezer, then leave for 1 hour until the mixture starts to freeze around the edges. Whisk the mixture to break down the ice crystals, return to the freezer for 1 hour more, then repeat the whisking.

2 Lightly oil a large loaf tin, ice-cream tub or food container, approximately 2 litres in capacity. Line with cling film. Using a fork, lightly crush half the raspberries with the reserved sugar.

3 Spoon one-third of the semi-frozen ice cream into the tin. Sprinkle over half the meringue pieces and half the crushed raspberries. Spoon over 3 tbsp coulis or sauce. Cover with another third of the ice cream and then the remaining meringues, raspberries and another 3 tbsp coulis or sauce. Pour over the remaining ice cream, then put in the freezer for at least 4 hours, or overnight.

4 Transfer the dessert to the fridge for 30–45 minutes to soften it. When ready to eat, turn the cake out onto a dish. Scatter the raspberries over, then cut into thick slices and serve with a little of the coulis or sauce.

About the editor

Sarah Giles's passion for cooking started with the encouragement of two 'fantastically inspirational' home economics teachers at school. Having learnt all the basic, essential recipes and good old-fashioned techniques from them, she went on to cook as a hobby for many years, eventually becoming a finalist on BBC's *MasterChef* in the early years of the show. She has worked as a journalist and editor on many different lifestyle and home-interest magazines and became Food Editor on *Easy Cook* in 2006 and then Editor in 2007.

'When I'm cooking, I like to make tasty, nutritious food without spending hours in the kitchen – and that's exactly what *Easy Cook* magazine is all about. This new book, *Easy Cook Express*, is a collection of all our favourite recipes, and it's designed to show just how easy – and how much fun – cooking can be.' *Sarah Giles*

Photography credits

BBC Books and *Easy Cook* magazine would like to thank the following people for providing photographs. While every effort has been made to trace and acknowledge all photographers, we should like to apologise should there be any errors or omissions.

Marie-Louise Avery 139, 153; Peter Cassidy 79, 146; Jean Cazals 108; Will Heap 34, 123, 171; William Lingwood 92, 168; Gareth Morgans 4bl, 10, 18, 43, 55, 83, 89, 96, 112, 115, 119, 158; David Munns 4br, 6-7, 37, 44, 46, 49, 52, 63, 68, 80, 85, 86, 95, 100, 128, 135, 157, 167, 176, 179; Myles New 4tr, 13, 14, 17, 21, 39, 56, 60, 76, 154, 172, 180; Michael Paul 59, 75; Lis Parsons 4tl, 40, 67, 90, 107, 132, 140, 149, 150, 161, 174; Simon Smith 103; Roger Stowell 131, 163, 164, 187; Simon Walton 72, 127, 136, 145; Philip Webb 111, 116; Simon Wheeler 71; Kate Whitaker 120, 124.

10 9 8 7 6 5 4 3 2 1

Published in 2012 BBC Books, an imprint of Ebury Publishing.
A Random House Group Company

Recipes and photographs © BBC Worldwide
Book design © Woodlands Books Ltd
With thanks to BBC *Good Food* magazine, in which these recipes previously appeared.

The Random House Group Limited Reg. No. 954009

Addresses for companies within the Random House Group can be found at: www.randomhouse.co.uk

A CIP catalogue record for this book is available from the British Library.

ISBN 978 1 849 90432 2

The Random House Group Limited supports The Forest Stewardship Council® (FSC®), the leading international forest certification organisation. Our books carrying the FSC label are printed on FSC® certified paper. FSC is the only forest certification scheme endorsed by the leading environmental organisations, including Greenpeace. Our paper procurement policy can be found at www.randomhouse.co.uk/environment

Project editor: Laura Higginson
Designer: Kathryn Gammon
Picture researcher: Gabby Harrington
Photography: see above

Colour origination by: AltaImage
Printed and bound in China by C&C Offset Printing Co., Ltd

To buy books by your favourite authors and register for offers, visit www.randomhouse.co.uk

FSC
www.fsc.org

MIX
Paper from
responsible sources
FSC® C008047